The Social & Organizational Context of Management Accounting

ADVANCED MANAGEMENT AND ACCOUNTING SERIES
———————— Series Editor: David Otley ————————

Other titles in the series

The Social & Organizational Context of Management Accounting

ANTHONY G. PUXTY
Department of Accounting and Finance
University of Strathclyde
Glasgow, Scotland, UK

Published in association with
The Chartered Institute of Management Accountants

ACADEMIC PRESS
Harcourt Brace & Company, Publishers
London   San Diego   New York
Boston   Sydney   Tokyo   Toronto

ACADEMIC PRESS LTD.
24/28 Oval Road,
London NW1 7DX

United States Edition published by
ACADEMIC PRESS INC.
San Diego, California 92101–4311

A catalogue record for this book is available from the British Library

ISBN 0–12–568660–9

Typeset by Photo·graphics, Honiton, Devon
Printed and bound in Great Britain by Mackays of Chatham plc, Chatham, Kent

Series Editor's Preface

David Otley
KPMG Peat Marwick Professor of Accounting
Lancaster University

A major problem for the management accounting teacher has been the selection of a suitable text for advanced courses. Although a number of very good texts exist, they typically do not include some topics that individual teachers wish to teach. On the other hand, they do include a considerable amount of material on topics that are unnecessary for a particular course. Students often feel that they have a poor deal in purchasing large and expensive texts that do not cover the whole of their course, yet include large amounts of extraneous material.

This series is an attempt to resolve this problem. It will consist of a set of slim volumes, each of which deals with a single topic in depth. A coherent course of study may therefore be built up by selecting just those topics which an individual course requires, so that the student has a tailor-made text for the precise course that is being taken. The texts are aimed primarily at final year undergraduate courses in accounting and finance, although many will be suitable for MBA and other postgraduate programmes. A typical final year advanced management accounting option course could be built around four or five texts, as each has been designed to incorporate material that would be taught over a period of a few weeks. Alternatively, the texts can be used to supplement a larger and more general textbook.

Each text is a free-standing treatment of a specific topic by an authoritative author. They can be used quite independently of each other, although it is assumed that an introductory or intermediate-level management accounting course has been previously taken. However, considerable care has been taken in the choice and specification of topics, to ensure that the texts mesh together without unnecessary overlap. It is therefore hoped that the series will provide a valuable resource for management accounting teachers, enabling them to design courses that meet precise needs whilst still being able to recommend required texts at an affordable price.

To the memory of my parents, Joan and Harry.
They were good people.

Contents

Preface and
Acknowledgements
(The Personal Part)

This book has proved almost impossible to write. It attempts to cover a vast sweep of literature in philosophy, the social sciences and management. Any few pages of the book represent a subject-matter that has been the focus of many books. If anyone might have had a hope of succeeding in writing the book, it should not have been an accountant. Yet linking this fascinating and yet maddening literature to accounting can only be managed by an accountant. That is why, despite the difficulties for writer and reader alike, the book had to be written: for there is now a large and growing accounting literature that stretches well beyond what has been the traditional source material for accounting theory – in particular, economics – and there is no guide through it. I hope that in a modest way, this book can act as such a guide. The book is addressed to students and those academic accountants wishing to learn where this literature is coming from, rather than my fellow explorers in the area. This disclaimer explains, I hope, why in a hundred and fifty pages or so, so much is missing.

The preface to any book is an occasion for self-indulgence. I propose to take advantage of this and indulge myself in acknowledging the help of the many colleagues who, over the years, have helped me to understand at least a small portion of what we should all as accounting academics know, and yet so few of us do know. They are not to blame for the bad bits; they can take credit for the good bits.

I joined the University of Sheffield in 1976. It was my first teaching job and it was unnerving. In that first year I learned more about my subject than I have ever done in a comparable period before or since. Credit for this goes entirely to Tony Lowe and Tony Tinker. They showed me something that was then hidden to most of us: that accounting is important in its ramifications and social impact, and that it is not just a collection of techniques. Nowadays this view is commonplace; then, it was a revelation. From them I learned what it means to be a committed academic who cares passionately about one's subject: and I learned what critical faculties are. In the case of Tony Lowe this extended to all aspects of one's life, and it was at times a painful experience. But, "no pain, no gain, Listy", as Rimmer said once in *Red Dwarf*. Knowing Tony Lowe was a unique experience.

Also at Sheffield, then and over the next few years I was fortunate to work with Wai Fong Chua, Colin Dodds, Trevor Hopper, Richard Laughlin, Peter Miller, John Oliga and Dick Wilson. Visiting tutors in the early years were David Cooper and David Otley. From outside the accounting group I learned much from Ankie Hoogvelt. Not all those in accounting were committed to the radical vision that was agreed to characterize Sheffield. Yet among those that were there was a commitment that was inspiring, and that I have since found in other areas of accounting and finance at the University of Strathclyde. Together, Tony, Richard, Wai Fong and I especially, explored various radical theories, wrestling particularly with Habermas. We had little to help us; AOS was then still feeling its way too, and the university environment outside the accounting group was frequently hostile to the work we were doing. Tony's defence of his group in the face of opposition was a necessary condition for the explorations we undertook. It needed the strength of character that he had in abundance.

I overlapped with Tony Tinker for just the year 1976–7, after which he left for the USA. Wai Fong, Colin and Trevor left in the early 1980s and Peter Miller joined soon after. Then Tony Lowe took early retirement in 1985, and in 1987 I myself left to join the University of Strathclyde. Dick left around that time; Peter did too. Times had changed, and this mass exit was not coincidental. However, Richard Laughlin stayed on and has begun to build a new, different, but equally fascinating Sheffield from the ashes of the old. His personal qualities deserve the greatest admiration.

There are many others I must thank. The time spent working on the ESRC's Corporatism and Accountability project resulted in a close association with Hugh Willmott, David Cooper and Keith Robson. I should like to thank them for the always stimulating discussions we had while hammering out where that very large project should go next, even if I am still not sure where it did go. Towards the end of that project Prem Sikka became tangentially involved, and since then I have watched and tried to help in the arena of practical politics as he has demonstrated a tenacity that is exemplary, while at the same time becoming abundantly fluent and theoretically creative.

Ed Arrington visited Strathclyde in 1989–90. I learned more from him in the course of that year than from anybody else since the two Tonys. Thanks, Ed. After that I came to know Delia and Keith Pheby. Their passion and articulate knowledge of philosophy are rare in academia, and even more rare in accounting. I hope I am now beginning to get some understanding of the full ramifications of poststructuralism and postmodernism. If I am, credit is due to Ed, Delia and Keith.

More recently I have worked closely on a number of papers with Christine Cooper. Her commitment and insight have been a delight, and from her I have learned by observation how academic writing can be intertwined with one's being. I count it a privilege to work with her. This is also the place to thank my current colleagues for their tolerance towards those of us who are ploughing a different furrow from them. Not everybody could manage it with a smile.

There have of course been many others from whom I have learned, though not working directly with them. Notable in this category is Anthony Hopwood, whose conversations at European meetings were always stimulating, and who was always willing to cover written drafts with perceptive comments; and Marilyn Neimark and Cheryl Lehman, who have been such good colleagues stateside. Others with whom I have enjoyed insightful discussions include Peter Armstrong, Pat Arnold, Theresa Hammond, Keith Hoskin, Leslie Oakes, Fahrettin Okcabol, Mike Power and Paul Williams. I am sure there are many others who should be included here: I thank them all.

Practical acknowledgements are due, too. Various parts of the manuscript have been read by Christine Cooper, David Otley, and Tony Tinker. Hugh Willmott deserves especially grateful thanks for having the patience to look over most of it, and for making such perceptive comments. They are not of course responsible for any oddities or idiosyncrasies remaining. I'd like to thank Ed who suggested the title to Chapter 5, and Ian Craib, since I shamelessly adapted a chapter title to his book for my own title to Chapter 6. I must thank David Otley (again) for asking me to write this book, and both David and Jennifer Pegg for their patience. Jennifer's faxes in particular have been a model of good-mannered persistence in the face of repeatedly missed deadlines. I hope the result is worth the wait.

I should like to reserve my final thanks for a certain overseas university which turned me down when I applied for a senior lectureship back in 1982. No worries, sports. They ensured that I remained in the uniquely stimulating atmosphere of Sheffield.

Helensburgh

Introduction

This book is concerned with the foundations of thought that underlie much modern social and organizational research in accounting. It is not intended to be a textbook that recounts the "discoveries" and full arguments of all the papers that have appeared under this heading – there is not room. It is, rather, intended as an introduction to the philosophical and social theories that underlie much recent accounting research. In broad terms I have structured the book within each of the four central chapters into, first, the philosophical foundations of the approach taken: and then some accounting papers from within the tradition to exemplify the way these foundations are expressed in the accounting literature itself. There will not, normally, be a straightforward one-to-one correspondence between the accounting papers discussed and the "foundation literature" underlying them. Overall, it is best to see my discussions of the foundation literature as a bridge between the real thing and the way accountants have made use of it.

This approach has its dangers. To attempt to collapse the richness of the social sciences generally and those of 100 or more accounting papers in particular into a short book like this can only be misleading. The book is therefore intended as a guide through a literature which can be tough to understand at times. It should help the reader of the papers in the literature both to see links among papers and also to understand how authors can write what they do (i.e. it explains the way writing always takes place within traditions of thought and world views). I have assumed throughout that the reader will look at the original accounting papers directly, whether or not they also look at some of the philosophical and social science work discussed.

The book is intended for two main audiences. First, for third- and fourth-year students, or those on masters or doctoral programmes who wish to know what is happening outside the traditional confines of economics-based accounting research; and second, to my academic colleagues who would like to explore this literature and who might find a guide through it helpful. No knowledge is assumed of the reader beyond a knowledge of traditional management accounting, and some knowledge of traditional management accounting research. Little or no knowledge of the other social sciences is assumed (although no doubt most readers will be familiar with economics!).

As stated, I deal with the foundations that underlie the approaches to management accounting recently taken, and this will entail forays into philosophy, sociology, political theory, literary theory, and economics. There are at least two dangers in dealing with massive areas such as this in such brief detail. First, simplification is necessary, to the point at which ideas seem either simple when they are not, or trite when they are not. Second, there is a danger of missing the debates in these areas: for what are presented as "given" ideas are often the subject of fierce disagreements among those closely associated with the ideas. Much of this richness must inevitably be lost. What will be gained, hopefully, is a better understanding of the turn that has been taken in management accounting research over the past ten years.

Accounting texts do not fall into particular boxes, fitting neatly into the chapter outline that I have constructed. They do not in general attach themselves to a paradigm. Each is an individual piece of work that reflects the thoughts and judgements of its authors: and these authors may well combine insights from different schools of thought. I state this because I have observed that most writers do not like being labelled: because among other things, labelling can imply a straitjacket ("I vow not to move outside my appointed paradigm") and a lack of original thought ("Here is the master; I am but a poor accounting puzzle-solver"). Nevertheless, if a piece of accounting work seems to me to fall squarely into a particular school of thought, then I say so. Without classification we are left with a body of literature that is even more difficult to unravel.

I have learned a great deal from writing this little book, and enjoyed the task much of the time. I hope some of this transmits itself to you.

1

The Received Wisdom

"Agency theory is just Hobbes in drag."

– Ed Arrington

INTRODUCTION

Every subject is governed by its framework. Whatever is said or written is the result of a series of presuppositions.

Sometimes presuppositions are stated explicitly. In his geometry, Euclid explains the postulates and axioms that will be supposed – for example, that a straight line is the shortest distance between two points, or that parallel lines never meet. In neoclassical economics the assumptions about individual rationality are generally clearly stated, such as transitivity of choices in a preference ordering, and intertemporal consistency.

Often, however, the assumptions a writer makes are not clearly stated. There are a number of possible reasons for this. One might be a conviction on the part of the writer that it is unnecessary to enumerate the assumptions, because they are "obvious", and that the reader shares the assumptions and likewise considers them to be obvious. A second possible reason is that the writer is not aware of the assumptions being made. They are so natural to the writer, and to the context in which the writer thinks and works, that a questioning of them does not arise.

Clearly, if we look at any individual text by a given writer it is difficult to disentangle either of these explanations from the

3

other. To give an example of this, let us take a well-known UK management accounting textbook. We do not choose this book because it is a poor book: on the contrary, more care has been taken in this book than most similar texts to think through the approach taken and the reasoning presented to the reader. The book is *Accounting for Management Decisions*, by John Arnold and Tony Hope (1983). The first chapter of the book begins (p. 3) with the following words:

> This is a book about accounting. Specifically it is a book about one area of accounting, often called *management accounting* or *managerial accounting*, which is concerned with the provision of information to those responsible for managing businesses and other economic organizations to help them in making decisions about the future of the organization and in controlling the implementation of the decisions they make.

This is not an unusual approach: it is an approach taken, explicitly or implicitly, by all modern management accounting textbooks. In beginning their book, Arnold and Hope provide us with a definition of management accounting. Yet this is not the only conceivable approach to a definition. To illustrate, let us give two other possible definitions of management accounting. Here is the first:

Management accounting is a set of social practices that delineate the space within which the activity of the workforce might be made visible and susceptible to rational calculation.

Here is the second:

Management accounting is an instrument within an enterprise that facilitates the exploitation of, and extraction of surplus value from, its employees by the capitalist interests that, through management, control the accounting system.

You will see immediately that each of these definitions differs substantively from the other: and both differ substantially from the definition given by Arnold and Hope. None of these definitions is self-evidently right. None of them is free of the values held by those who propose them. All of them can only be understood in the context of the web of beliefs and reasoned arguments that constitute the framework from which they come.

Nor must it be assumed that the definitions are mutually exclusive. In saying that there are different approaches that can be taken to defining a subject, and hence providing a framework for it, we are not implying that each approach is discrete and in opposition to other approaches. We can exemplify this through the above definitions. Management accounting may, at the same time, help capitalist interests control the workforce (the third definition) and help management in making decisions (Arnold and Hope's approach). A definition defines the space within which more detailed analysis takes place; in doing so it certainly excludes other spaces: but it does not carve out for itself a wholly unique space.

That is the basic message of this book. The traditional framework is not necessarily the "obvious" one, still less is it obviously the correct or the objective one. There are different ways of looking at management accounting in organizations. All of them can be consistent and wholly justifiable, given that their own frameworks are themselves justifiable. This means that, to understand management accounting and to understand the research literature in management accounting, it is necessary to understand the assumptions and reasoning behind the various frameworks that have driven management accounting research over the past two decades. Only from this position can any evaluation be made: only from this position can a reasoned argument be sustained about what management accounting "really" is. As a result, we shall be concerned in this book with the frameworks themselves: with the rationales behind them, with the propositions they contain, with the differences between them, and with critical comment on them. You should not look here for a prescription on "how to do management accounting better". You should, it is hoped, emerge from reading it with a critical eye for what you are told about the nature of management accounting, and with an ability to understand the social research literature that has grown over the past few years that concerns itself with management accounting practices.

Let us pursue a little further, however, the reason why this approach is so unusual, and why most of the texts you have met or will meet make no mention of this. Writings in management accounting arise from traditions. The authors of textbooks, monographs and academic papers all work from within the traditions that have governed their writers. Arnold and Hope (1983), already mentioned, gives more attention than many texts to the LSE economics tradition. Wilson and Chua (1988) take an organizational control perspective. Sizer (1989) is founded on the conventional approach of the professional management accountant. In what they write the authors express the beliefs and expound the principles and practices that have been taught to them, that are espoused by their immediate colleagues, and/or that they believe do or should constitute the practices of corporate management accountants in their day-to-day operations.

As a result there is a considerable consistency in the content of most management accounting writings. Textbooks cover much the same ground (budgets; cost apportionment; standard costing; CVP analysis, and so on). Academic articles tend to be within easily-identifiable traditions, and investigate well-recognized research topics. We shall call this a *paradigm:*[1] and hence, we shall refer to conventional management accounting as the *traditional paradigm.* The traditional paradigm has philosophical roots in just the same way as the schools of thought considered in subsequent chapters, and we shall discuss these presently.

We shall begin, however, by considering the wide variety of approaches to management accounting that we typify under the heading of the traditional paradigm. We shall then consider in detail the various characteristics that are typical of the traditional paradigm. Each of the approaches outlined later in this book challenges at least one of these characteristics. Finally in this chapter we shall dig a little more deeply into the philosophical roots of conventional management accounting.

MANAGEMENT ACCOUNTING RESEARCH AND PRACTICE WITHIN THE TRADITIONAL PARADIGM

In the field of accounting theory, developments have taken place very quickly. It is only perhaps in the past thirty years that a serious theoretical literature has developed: and it has developed with such speed, and with so many changes of direction, that easily-recognized names for schools of thought have not grown commensurately with it. In this section then we shall describe approaches to theory and practice with labels for the purpose of

---

[1] In using the term "paradigm" we are not necessarily using it in the Kuhnian (1970) sense. Much has been written about the inappropriateness of Kuhn's work to a social science such as accounting (cf. Laughlin, 1981). We do not propose to compound the error here: merely to use it in the looser sense of an agreed framework within which authors operate.

future reference within this book, even though they might be challenged by those conducting the work.

The following approaches are those that we propose to consider as falling within the traditional accounting paradigm.[2] You may find Table 1.1 helpful in summarizing the next few pages.

Management accounting practice as described by the traditional teaching textbook

This is a heading that will be readily recognized by all readers. Traditional textbooks have settled into a list of topics that, despite the lesser differences in orientation mentioned earlier, are common to all. The overall purpose of these books is to describe means of using financial calculation for control and unprogrammed decision-making. The content is a list of techniques that are expected to achieve this: for instance, identifying cost objects, CVP relationships, cost allocation and apportionment, job-order and process costing, standard costing, budget systems, capital budgeting, and so on.

The application of mathematical models to traditional techniques

The 1960s and 1970s saw a massive effort to refine traditional calculation using mathematical and statistical analysis. A good summary of this literature can be found in Bhaskar (1981). Bhaskar's headings are (amended): cost–volume–profit analysis as related to portfolio analysis and utility analysis; financial simulation models; cost allocation as related to mathematical programming, input–output analysis and game theory; cost variance investigation modelling; mathematical modelling for control, short-run decisions, long-run planning and transfer pricing. The common purpose of these models is much the same as that of traditional textbook techniques.

Behavioural accounting

A further major theoretical development has been the extensive empirical and theoretical attention to the effects of accounting

---

[2] The reader will notice that agency theory is omitted from this list. This may at first be surprising, given that it figures extensively in the mainstream literature. We do not consider agency theory to conform to the criteria considered in this chapter.

TABLE 1.1 Management accounting approaches.

	Traditional texts	Mathematical modelling	Behavioural accounting	HIPS	Anthony framework	Strategic accounting
Empirical testing?	of little importance	of little importance	important	important	not important	not important
Assumed social structure	markets	mostly markets	mostly markets	mostly bypasses the issue	markets	markets
Assumption of nature of man	individualistic utility-maximizing	generally individualistic utility-maximizing	complex man	mostly individualistic utility-maximizing	mostly individualistic utility-maximizing	less important to theory
Explicitly normative?	yes	mostly	sometimes	sometimes	mostly	frequently
Reductionist?	usually	yes	mostly	yes	to a limited extent	not much
Assumes closed system?	yes	yes	mostly	yes	to a limited extent	not much
Organizational/ managerial perspective?	yes	yes	yes	yes	yes	yes
Ahistorical?	yes	yes	yes	yes	yes	in most cases
Technical orientation?	yes	yes	yes	yes	yes	yes

systems on people, and the effects of people on accounting systems, using models from psychology and social psychology. The title usually given to this approach, behavioural accounting, is a most unfortunate one since pretty much *all* accounting practice and research is concerned with its relationship to human behaviour. However the designation is now common and we shall use it here for that reason only. An early summary of the research may be found in Hopwood (1974), though this is now seriously out of date; more recent reviews are to be found in Emmanuel and Otley (1985) particularly Chapters 3, 6, 7, and 8; and in Ezzamel and Hart (1987), especially Chapters 3, 4 and 15.

Human information processing (HIPS)

Originally perhaps a subset of behavioural accounting, this research has burgeoned in quantity, until it deserves a place on its own. Rooted in behavioural decision theory, which itself relies heavily on cognitive psychology and statistical method, this set of research homes in on the individual decision-maker faced with accounting information. A full, though now dated, summary of the whole HIPS field may be found in Libby (1981); a more recent, brief, UK summary that is focused on management accounting is contained in Ezzamel and Hart (1987), Chapter 5.

Anthony's planning and control theory

A significant influence on management accounting thought has been the classification method used by Robert Anthony of Harvard (cf. Anthony, 1965, 1988) which has now reached into many traditional (and not-so-traditional) accounting texts. Taking management control to be a branch of social psychology, it has developed a demarcation of management control from strategic control and operational control that has placed management accounting firmly as a function of the third (although it might be argued that cost accounting *per se* relates to both management control and operational control).

Strategic management accounting

We use this label to cover two schools of development from the 1980s. One does indeed describe itself as strategic management accounting, and is heavily indebted to Kenneth Simmonds at the London Business School (cf. Simmonds, 1981; Bromwich, 1990). The other is one that has recently taken an interest in developing new cost control and decision methods, and is associated particularly with the names of Robert Kaplan, Thomas Johnson and Robin Cooper. It claims to be contextualized in the markets and technologies of today, particularly stimulated by Japanese business methods (see Johnson and Kaplan, 1987; Cooper and Kaplan, 1987, etc.).

THE CHARACTERISTICS OF THE TRADITIONAL PARADIGM

We turn now to the characteristics that are in most cases common to the above approaches to management accounting but which are challenged in the approaches to be considered in the subsequent chapters of this book.

It is framed from the perspective of the organization

As we have seen, the normal approach to management accounting is to acknowledge that it takes place within a business organization. The step that follows immediately from this is to suppose that, because management accounting takes place within the organization, therefore matters concerning management accounting should be considered from the point of view of the organization. Thus, when a feature is discussed, its nature is perceived from within a managerial/organizational perspective (that is, the perspectives of the management as a whole and of the organization are treated as indistinguishable). Definition of problems, and evaluation of solutions, are both generated from the organization's viewpoint.

A simple example will suffice. During the 1970s a literature burgeoned that looked at budgeting behaviour by members of the organization, both "budgetees" and those they are responsible to. A phrase grew up with this literature: "dysfunctional behaviour". Now dysfunction is generally taken to mean, in effect, harmful. The literature defined this term as being what appears to be harmful to the organization. For instance, budget biasing (in particular, the creation of slack in the setting of the budget) was generally seen as dysfunctional because, as a result, the organization might not be able to lead the manager towards making the effort that would be good for the organization.

Yet this is not the only conceivable approach: the exact opposite could equally well be taken as a starting point. Rather than define dysfunction in the organization's terms we could define it in the budgetee's terms. Dysfunctions would then be those organizational actions that further restricted the choice, action or happiness of the manager: and the good of the individual manager would be the criterion. Yet another approach would be to banish the whole notion of dysfunction, from either point of view, and instead view each as a phenomenon to be studied: nothing more nor less. It will be observed that the very term "bias" in budget bias is itself value-laden and appears to imply something wrong: that is, the use of the term implies that there is a true and correct figure from which some process or structure has created a distortion. The reader who doubts this is invited to imagine the phrase, "You are biased" as a neutral term or as offering praise. The implication is that, when the conventional literature considers the notion of bias, it may or may not prescriptively state that there should be ways of reducing or eliminating the bias; but whether or not this is made explicit, the implication is left hanging in the air, by the very term used – "bias" – that it is undesirable.

We can understand further the implicit managerialism of the standard literature by considering the topics that are the standard subject of research and of inclusion in syllabuses and textbooks. These include, for instance, standard costing; and no purpose of standard costing is envisaged except as a teleological tool: one to reduce cost through indicating variances to be investigated. The reader will look in vain for, for example, a discussion of the stress and illness (as dysfunction!) to the budgetee caused by the use of standard cost and budget variance control systems.

It treats the organization as effectively a closed system

The social and economic worlds are highly complex; and one aspect of that complexity is the interaction of each element of the world with others. The difference in approach that this causes can be seen in the method used to introduce the subject of economics to new readers. Economics texts frequently used to begin to explain neoclassical concepts through a discussion of Robinson Crusoe (cf. Speight, 1960, Chapter 3) – simplifying as a starting point by indicating Crusoe's needs. They no longer do so: and this is a tacit recognition that economic behaviour is essentially just one aspect of social behaviour, and that to take a Robinson Crusoe in isolation is only to distort what is going on in real economies.

Both individuals and organizations interact with their environments, and it is only in that interaction that they can be properly understood. A characteristic of conventional management accounting is that it tends both to ignore the existence of the environment of the organization, and to ignore the interaction among the various elements of the organization. (We say "tends" here, because some parts of the traditional paradigm have a greater tendency to this than others. Mathematical modelling is very prone to it. Strategic management accounting is relatively free of it.)

Again, an example would be helpful. Take cost–volume–profit analysis in the multiproduct firm. It is generally acknowledged that CVP analysis is unhelpful in such organizations, for a good reason: it depends crucially on the distinction between fixed and variable costs, and hence the attribution of these costs to each product to be analysed. In a multiproduct firm the problem of cost apportionment arises, which must always be solved in some arbitrary fashion, as a result of which a CVP analysis for an individual product must be meaningless. Nevertheless, it is frequently undertaken, with a supposition such as assuming that the product mix stays constant. Yet the whole point of the analysis is to understand the cost–profit behaviour of an individual product under different output conditions – in other words, where the product mix does not remain constant!

This deals with the interaction among the various parts of the organization. But what about the organization's interaction with other organizations? Again, traditional costing ignores them. For example, consider pricing models. These link cost to price for the individual product. They rarely or never build in the dynamics that result from the change in price that results from a change in cost. Such a price change may well (depending on market conditions) lead to price changes in competing organizations which in turn potentially lead to output changes and hence cost changes: but these interactions are omitted from the models.

A third example would be the corpus of HIPS research. Being concerned with the individual decision-maker, it explicitly eschews the relationships between the {cue → action} of one individual and the reactions to that action within the environment of the decision-maker. For instance, studies of functional fixation stop at experimental results from the decision-maker's behaviour: the whole approach has no mechanism for dealing with the organizational effects of functional fixation.[3]

---

[3] HIPS theorists might get hot under the collar at this point. This, they would say, is not their problem, and can be researched within a separate framework. HIPS cannot be blamed for not doing what it does not claim to do. I agree: but nobody seems to do such research. Anyway, I am not explicitly criticizing HIPS here, just pointing to its limiting characteristics.

It has a technical orientation

It is best to begin here by defining what we mean by "technical". Certain aspects of human society are concerned with the achievement of what we might with Habermas call "strategic" ends. Rather than being ends in themselves (such as the appreciation of the beauty of a painting) they are concerned with a means–end calculus: what is good is that which is efficient. Indeed, it would be difficult to conceive of anyone supposing that "inefficiency" would be a good thing. Like the term "bias" that we discussed above, "efficiency" is a term that has emotive connotations. Yet it is one that leaves a great deal to be desired. For example, a factory producing poison gases for germ warfare might, by many, be considered undesirable in terms of human welfare: and in this case efficiency in producing the gases is not necessarily a matter for approval. In other words, we might argue that if we wish to evaluate an organizational process, we should do so in terms of the desirability of the ends, not of the way those ends are achieved without regard for what they are.

Traditional management accounting has no means of doing this. It has been designed, and is usually interpreted, in a way that is specifically geared towards evaluating only the technical efficiency of the process of producing something, rather than evaluating the totality.

This in turn is founded in the organizational/managerial orientation discussed earlier. The purpose of the business organization is infrequently challenged: instead it is accepted as a vehicle for the production of goods or services of some kind. Then, the criterion for the performance of that entity, and by implication the purpose of the management accounting system, is the effectiveness or efficiency with which it achieves this. But this partition is a dangerous one. If a dictator were determined to kill some of his subjects, we would not congratulate him if he were able to do so at a lower cost. Yet management accounting, as it is generally defined, can only do precisely this: and it does so because it defines its purpose in terms of the managerial task, which itself is not open to question. Others set the objectives (such as, in the traditional model, wealth maximization for the owners) and managers may not enquire beyond its successful achievement. As their instrument, management accounting too cannot enquire any further.

It is prescriptive

Given that we have already pointed to the managerialist orientation of management accounting, it will not be surprising that the rationale for it is that it can prescribe better methods of doing things. The reader is invited to turn to a standard management accounting text. It will be seen that, generally, the descriptive is indistinguishable from the prescriptive, so that the reader is never sure if the technique being described is one that is used in practice, or one that is not used but, the author feels, should be used. Either way, it is rare to find criticism of a technique that is taught: and even where there is such criticism (and some authors are willing to criticize, say, absorption costing), there is still a prescription, namely, not to do what is being done.[4]

This raises a broader attribute which is characteristic of most Western thought. The world is seen as voluntaristic: as manipulable by people so as to improve some aspect of life. There is, in short, a belief in progress. The world may be made better, and it may be improved by human action. Words such as "fate" or "destiny" have almost dropped out of our vocabulary. Management accounting has become taken-for-granted as part of the toolbox that can enable this process of improvement to take place.

It is ahistorical

There are many ways into analysis in social science. One distinction is between cross-sectional and historical analysis. The first of these attempts to explain what is found by reference to other features, either of the entity being investigated, or of the environment of that entity. The second of these attempts to explain features through their history: they are as they are because of previous developments. The two are not, of course, wholly mutually exclusive, but there is a tendency in cross-sectional analysis to ignore the historical, far more than the tendency in historical analysis to ignore the context.

There are many good examples of this in the behavioural budgeting literature. Stedry's (1960) model, for instance, is closed-

---

[4] This raises a fairly complex issue. As we shall suggest later in this chapter, the traditional paradigm generally supposes the strict distinction between fact and value, between what is and what ought to be, following the precepts of the philosopher David Hume. Albeit unintentionally, the fuzzing of these boundaries by conventional texts places them outside the realm of conventional Anglo-Saxon thought.

system but also ahistorical: it makes no attempt to explain people's choices as a result of their previous experiences. The same may be said of Hofstede (1967), Ronen and Livingstone (1975) and Hopwood (1974). To take the last-named, for example, we find that there appears on the surface to be a time dimension, in that the manager employing a "profit-conscious style" takes a longer-term criterion than the "budget-constrained style". This, however, is not in itself an acknowledgement of the historical, since there is no consideration of the evolution of these styles.

It is apolitical

When we say that the traditional paradigm is "apolitical", we must not be misunderstood. We are not suggesting that traditional management accounting successfully avoids political issues in society: rather, we are suggesting that it implicitly *claims* to avoid these issues, whereas it is no more able to avoid them than any other social phenomenon.

There are perhaps two schools of thought here (other than, of course, those who believe that accounting remains wholly politically neutral: Professor Solomons thinks it should be). One is that accounting itself is politically engaged. The other is that accounting is not in itself political, but that because political issues pervade the social world in which accounting operates, it thereby becomes intertwined with the political. Briefly, the first may be justified by pointing to the accountability dimension of accounting, and arguing that accountability cannot be separated from hierarchy. Hierarchy in turn implies a relationship of power, and power relations are by definition political. The second may be justified by suggesting that accountability relations are not necessarily linked to a rigid hierarchy: for instance, a manager in a workers' co-operative, or a vicar in a church, may both be accountable to (respectively) those they organize and their parishioners. Yet there is no reason why there should not be accounting reports to these parties even though the power relation is reciprocal.

As we pointed out earlier, the traditional paradigm is founded in the managerial perspective: and this factor alone is sufficient to implicate managerial accounting politically – at least, so long as one acknowledges that all interests in the organization are not congruent with management's interests.

It is rationalistic

There are many models of the nature of human action and judgement. The economist's model is the extreme which assumes rationality. Psychoanalytic models are perhaps the opposite extreme and suggest the crucial significance of the unconscious in affecting action.[5] Most models implicitly fall between these two extremes.

Traditional accounting models tend strongly towards the economic view. Accounting is treated as the quintessence of rational calculation. Those in control of the information use it rationally in making resource allocation decisions: those subject to its surveillance make rational decisions about their action based on their awareness of that surveillance (as, for instance, where the budgetee attempts to keep expenditure within the prescribed limits precisely because he or she supposes that rational decisions will be based on the presence or absence of variances).

The assumption of rationality may be seen in the studies on budget systems (for instance, in budget biasing studies); in traditional costing literature; in the mathematical modelling literature (it is fascinating to re-read this literature for the occasional *obiter dicta* recognizing that practising managers are oblivious to such models); in HIPS modelling;[6] and in strategic management accounting. It is, moreover, arguable that part at least of the accounting literature on ambiguity and choice (contrast Dyckman, 1981 with Cooper, Hayes and Wolf, 1981, and March, 1987) still betrays a yearning for rationality, while recognizing the difficulties of the model.

It is functionalist

Many terms in social science are subject to different interpretations, and functionalism is no exception. We shall give here a brief and somewhat crude explanation of a (hopefully) common use of the term.

A major problem for sociology and anthropology has been to account for the existence and persistence of particular institutions or phenomena. Not only does an institution such as marriage exist in a given society, for instance, it also persists over a long

---

[5] Cf. Freud (1920) on the death instinct and Jung (1944) on the significance of myth.
[6] HIPS does not of course suppose omniscience: that is its rationale. It does, however, take bounded rationality as a starting point. It is the touchstone of the rational that enables HIPS to develop findings that contrast with it.

period of time. How should this be explained? One approach might be to try to understand social features through historical enquiry: through using a historical method to explain the phenomenon under question, the analyst looks to its past to see how it has evolved into its present state. For example, to explain the current rituals and customs surrounding marriage, one looks to past rituals and customs and their gradual (and perhaps not so gradual) change over time.

However, this approach poses at least two problems. First, the historical record is often non-existent, sketchy or unreliable. Second, even where we know what a phenomenon changed from, and what it changed into, we still do not know why it changed in that way and not some other. To explain this, we need some conception of "social fit": the institution changed the way it did because that suited the interlocking social institutions.

Marriage is now as it is because of other social institutions such as religion (many weddings take place in church); fashion in formal dress (men mostly wear suits, women dresses); and the State (which registers marriages, even outside church weddings).

However, this leads to a further implication: that the institution could not have changed any other way. Any other form is inconceivable because it would not mesh with those other institutions so well. This effectively leads to a theoretical situation where, it turns out, we can forget the past and concentrate on cross-sectional functional analysis. Put simply and, no doubt, outrageously over-simply: an institution is the way it is because that suits the rest of the social system. If for any reason it fails in future to suit the system, we shall find it adapts. Then under the new situation, we shall still have a functionalist explanation, that is, an explanation in terms of the function the institution serves in the context of the society in which it is found. Things are the way they are because they could not survive any other way.

On the face of it this is a very powerful theoretical structure. However there are many criticisms of functionalism, and we shall consider these in Chapter 2. For now, we need only understand the nature of the argument.

The traditional accounting paradigm is functionalist. The management accounting textbook in particular is largely satisfied with the techniques described within. The fact that standard costing, for instance, has survived for a half-century is implicit evidence that it is beneficial. We justify the technique, in other words, in a kind of Darwinian sense. The justification seems to run like this: only the fittest techniques survive; costing techniques have survived: therefore costing techniques deserve to survive and hence are beneficial. Behavioural budgeting is similarly content to describe the way techniques fit into their organizational contexts: and the very use of the term "dysfunctional" (already discussed) as a term of criticism leads to the conclusion that techniques are judged in terms of their functions for other facets of the organization.

It is reductionist

As with other terms we use here, "reductionism" has more than one meaning in philosophy and social science. We shall use it here to indicate the belief that the phenomena relevant to an object of study can be meaningfully restricted to a proper subset of the actual set of phenomena. This is best understood through examples from accounting.

The traditional accounting paradigm is reductionist in two ways. First, the only phenomena that are ultimately considered to be significant are economic phenomena. This is not, of course, to suggest that insights from other academic disciplines are not employed: increasingly, they are. Although the most traditional tools of cost accounting were just a set of logical protocols to calculate and control economic outcomes, later work that developed within the paradigm did indeed borrow from other disciplines, first statistical and mathematical, later psychological and social psychological. But these insights were used only as a means towards the end of rational economic calculation. If social psychology was used to understand budget-setting behaviour, it was because the quality of the budget process appeared to lead to better or worse attainment of *economic* targets. If classical statistical theory was bolted on to CVP analysis, it was because this improved *economic* decision-making. There is, of course, an alternative, which would acknowledge that our social world comprises other than economic levels and economic indicators of satisfaction. This is entirely missing.

Second, the traditional paradigm effectively supposes that social effects and social action can be reduced to individual effects and individual action. Much work is concerned with control over the individual on the supposition that optimizing a function with respect to the individual manager will optimize the function for the organization as a whole. Similarly at the next level, it supposes that optimizing a function for a particular organization will bring about further economic (and of course other) social welfare functions in society more generally.[7]

It is positivist

Positivism is another term with many shades of interpretation. It has been imported into (mainly financial) accounting theory during the past ten years with a particular set of self-defined meanings by a group of authors at the University of Rochester. We use it here in the way described by Giddens, who suggests it has two characteristics:

> First, a conviction that all "knowledge", or all that is to count as knowledge, is capable of being expressed in terms which refer in an immediate way to some reality or aspects of reality that can be apprehended through the senses. Second a faith that the methods and logical structure of science, as epitomized in classical physics, can be applied to the study of social phenomena.
>
> (Giddens, 1976, p. 130)

The first of these beliefs means that the traditional accounting paradigm concerns itself only with phenomena that are in principle or in practice measurable. They are measurable because they are accessible to our senses: we can listen to opinions in an interview, read responses in a questionnaire, observe the slope of a break-even chart. These phenomena can thus also be justified as relevant because they are *real*: nobody can accuse the positive analyst of supposing the existence of something that does not exist.

The second characteristic has led to a frequent requirement that traditional research should define variables with precision, measure them, and subject them to classical statistical tests. This leads to acceptance or rejection of hypotheses; it leads to associations of variables through regression models. Despite an acknowledgement that covariance does not in itself imply causality, it has also led to attempts to build causal models for organizational control (once again the behavioural budgeting literature provides many clear examples of this: so does prescriptive transfer pricing theory).

---

[7] An objection to this picture might be that there is a substantial transfer pricing literature concerned with the development of incentive systems so as to lead to goal congruence and hence harmony between individual goals and action and organizational goals. However the fact that this is one small part of the total picture of traditional techniques, added on to the others as a kind of "repair kit", is evidence of the lack of acknowledgement of this problem in the bulk of the traditional literature.

It is interesting to note that there was a brief flurry of research (Hayes, 1977) employing factor analysis. This was consistent with the second characteristic given here, but not with the first characteristic (since statistical factors are not perceivable by the senses). It is noteworthy that this method appears to have lost favour, perhaps for this reason.

It is problem-centred

The social world is a world of relationships, power, status, class, hierarchy, linguistic competence, symbol and myth. Its constituents are interactive and complex. The social, the political and the economic form a tightly woven web. Accounting phenomena are one part of this. They are of great interest in themselves, to be understood as part of our attempt to understand the social world in which we live, just the way that economics, politics, sociology and anthropology are studied.

However, traditional theory defines accounting phenomena solely in terms of problems to be solved. Accounting's roots lie in the instrumental: accounting is seen as a means to achieve an end. As a result, the phenomena that are considered within the traditional paradigm are restricted, in that characteristics that do not constitute problems are ignored: and those that do get considered are approached in a way that implies that there is something wrong, or potentially wrong, and which can be fixed.

This returns us to the point made earlier on p. 14, that accounting has traditionally tended to be optimistic in its view of human progress. It is founded on the supposition that it can, when applied judiciously, aid in the achievement of whatever is being sought. It will be noted, however, that this optimism concerning progress coexists with a certain pessimism about the human character: accounting's existence is also necessitated by the supposition that people will not improve their behaviour without the surveillance of an accounting system. People have failings as individuals – they will slack, or may make mistakes. A well-designed accounting system will help to rectify these failings by channelling people's energies into activities desirable to the organization.[8]

---

[8] As an aside, we may note a minor paradox here. The underlying philosophy of conventional accounting is individualistic (we shall have more to say about this presently). However, its function as a control mechanism is designed to support the aspirations of the collective (the business organization) *against* the individual (the potentially slacking budgetee).

THE PHILOSOPHICAL FOUNDATIONS OF THE TRADITIONAL PARADIGM

We now turn to investigate in more detail the most basic framework of thought that underlies the traditional accounting paradigm. Because the traditional paradigm is espoused by the majority of accounting practitioners, writers and thinkers, there is a tendency to suppose that it is "normal". The problem here is that the converse of "normal" is "abnormal": and once one begins thinking of alternative approaches to management accounting as abnormal, there is a tendency to suppose that their arguments may be dismissed as peripheral.

This is particularly so if it is supposed that, though these other approaches may have their roots in the abstract ideas of philosophers and social scientists, traditional theory is "common sense" and "obvious" and, as such, may be supposed to take precedence over other approaches which are "just" the thoughts or opinions of philosophers remote from the real world. In this final section we shall show that, on the contrary, the traditional approach is itself no more than a conflation of some of the precepts of particular philosophical schools. We may, indeed, paraphrase the well-known dictum of Keynes (1936) to suggest that "practical men, who believe themselves to be quite exempt from any intellectual influences are usually the slaves of some defunct philosopher".[9] The same statement may be made concerning traditional academic theorists (although we trust they do not consider themselves wholly exempt from any intellectual influences).

Before we begin, it is as well to make a disclaimer. The following must not be taken as a Cook's tour of the history of some part of political philosophy and the philosophy of social science. In such a brief space this would be quite impossible (as well as presumptuous). It is only intended as an indicator of the directions taken by past thinkers that have formed themselves into the foundations of thought that govern conventional management accounting theory and practice today.

---

[9] This is no doubt unfair: the philosophers discussed are major figures in our intellectual history and by no means "defunct". However, they are far from being unchallengeable, and the purpose of this book is to indicate the nature of those challenges.

Philosophy of society or philosophy of knowledge?

Some readers may object that, in the chapter so far, I have conflated at least three separate issues. First, there is practice itself. Second, there is the normative academic literature, which suggests how practice should be. Third, there is the descriptive academic literature, testing hypotheses about how things are. Each of these should need separate analysis because they are so very different in themselves. The first and second should be linked because their roots lie in political philosophy: because what we find, and what we recommend, are both predicated on the social configuration and the role of accounting in that configuration. Taking elements of functionalism as described earlier, the argument would go that accounting is the way it is because that has been demanded by its social context (which more specifically may be taken to be a business context, though that is more problematic). Thus, to locate accounting practice and improvements to it, we need to understand the society in which it operates.

However (to continue the hypothetical objection) this is quite distinct from the descriptive aspect of accounting literature, where (for instance) the investigator attempts to make sense of accounting practices by running statistical tests on its relationship to the appropriate contextual variables. For this, a philosophical foundation in scientific method is relevant. A methodological investigation is the proper one.

Although political philosophy and the philosophy of science (or social science) are distinct, this distinction cannot be sustained. Although it is perfectly true that many volumes exist on each of these topics, this is for epistemological convenience, not because there is a clear distinction between them. A thinker's political beliefs and political recommendations tend to be intertwined with his or her views on the nature of the world; and these in turn are intertwined with his or her beliefs about the appropriate way to investigate how the world is. Although we cannot fully substantiate this statement right now, three brief and arguably simplistic examples will illustrate the point. John Locke (1632–1704) was probably the earliest philosopher to argue for democratic liberalism.[10] He was also the leading member of the British

---

[10] It must be said that, writing as he did in the context of the seventeenth century, Locke's notion of the meaning of democracy differed substantially from ours. Nevertheless he did argue strongly for the rights of the individual under God, and for a person's right to liberty so long as his actions do not infringe the rights of others.

empiricist school of philosophy, believing in the primacy of sense data/evidence in gaining knowledge of the world. Karl Marx (1818–83) argued that democratic liberalism was inevitably a sham, because it gave licence to some to exploit others, and that this could be understood through the class-based nature of society. Marx's method rejects sense data as evidence because the way in which it is organized by the investigator will be affected by the ideology that results from the class system. More recently, Karl Popper (b. 1902) has attacked the political philosophy of Plato, Hegel and Marx for, among other things, its totalitarian notion of social design, arguing instead for incrementalism (that is, sustaining a critical eye to find faults in individual parts of society and then sorting out those political problems piecemeal). This is consistent with Popper's methodological falsificationism, which is dependent on continued criticism of ideas put forward in the realm of scientific knowledge.

With these points in mind, let us turn to see the extent to which individualistic market philosophy on the one hand, and empiricist methodology on the other, are common sense propositions.

A brief history of individualism and empiricism

To suppose that any proposition is "normal" and "common sense" we have to suppose that it is time-invariant: that what is now common sense has always been common sense. Once we abandon this belief, and acknowledge that common sense, far from being common to all eras, it itself a socially determined way of thinking, we can no longer sustain it as being "obvious". Thus, to anyone with any scientific knowledge at all, it is "obvious" that, in a gravity-free vacuum with zero friction, an object once in motion will continue with a uniform velocity and constant direction for ever. This was not common sense at all until Galileo overturned the Aristotelian view of dynamics. For Aristotle, things *naturally* slowed down and stopped (an any rate, on earth), unless something kept moving them.

We may then show that the views we wish to examine are not, in themselves, ones that occur naturally to people. That free product and labour markets are relatively new in the economic history of the world should not come as any surprise to the reader: these mechanisms were unknown until the current millennium, and then developed only slowly in the feudal era, flourishing only with the rise of capitalism. However, two other propositions are equally distinctive in modern thought. One is that the individual is the natural starting point for discussions of the nature of society – a necessary starting point, given an accounting that relies on individual welfare through market mechanisms. The other is that the individual has rights quite separate from those given by God, and that these may include property rights.

Early political theory, notably that of Plato, surprises the modern reader precisely because it pays so little attention to the individual as a unit of analysis. Plato's political method is to propose an ideal State. Later idealists might propose ideal States to increase human liberty or human happiness. This is alien to the thinking of Plato (and Aristotle): they are concerned, rather, with justice (which does not mean to them precisely what it means to us) and with the good and virtuous life. The Republic of Plato, then, was a State designed to survive and to further the good (which generally meant the contemplative) life. Aristotle's *Politics*, for example, viewed the State's purpose as being to produce people with certain social skills and beliefs. Rather than the State existing for the person, the person was the product of the State. "Human need" was wholly absent from Greek concerns.

Nor were concerns of liberty, of freedom to conduct life as one chooses, or freedom from hunger or misery, central to the thought of later philosophers from the time of the Greeks until the seventeenth century. To the Greeks it was taken for granted that association among men[11] was central to the nature of man. It would not have occurred to them to question this. To later Christian philosophers, the spiritual glue joining God to man was such that, similarly, other such approaches would have been inconceivable. The virtuous life was still the fundamental concern of philosophy: though now it was the life pleasing to God within the context of received Christian doctrine.

The first break with this tradition came with the writings of Francis Bacon (1561–1626), who insisted on the clear distinction between matters of nature and matters of theology. The former was to be the subject of experimental knowledge: the latter the domain of faith. It must be emphasized that the notion of careful scientific observation, still more experimentation, was a novel

---

[11] I use this term for the remainder of this chapter, because historically "man" meant "men". To write "people" would not represent truly the spirit of the male-dominated philosophies of the past.

one.[12] Galileo (1564–1642) was the first major experimental scientist.[13]

This acknowledgement of the separation of the sacred from the secular in scientific knowledge was mirrored by the secularization of political thought. This is most evident in the work of Hobbes (1588–1679). Hobbes was the first political philosopher to begin from the premiss that the individual was the point from which analysis of society and the State should begin: the first to suppose that the basic state of nature was the man, alone. Hobbes's starting point then was the question: given that the State tends to restrict the individual's freedom to do what he wishes, why should men join together to form the State and acknowledge their subservience to it?

Hobbes's detailed answer need not concern us; though his pessimistic supposition that without the State man was forever at war with himself is interesting, since its depiction of man as fundamentally self-centred is echoed in the traditional accounting paradigm's supposition that administrative controls are necessary to ensure that the otherwise self-centred accountee attends to needs other than his own. What is important is Hobbes's willingness to abstract his argument from the notion of original

---

[12] Somewhere in his extensive writings, Russell points out that Aristotle, among the most revered of philosophers throughout the ages, remarked that women have fewer teeth than men. This could easily have been empirically tested, says Russell, by asking Mrs Aristotle to open her mouth while he counted her teeth. In a different vein, the words of Galen, the Greek second century physician, were so revered up to the time of Vesalius and Harvey in the sixteenth century, that his obviously erroneous statements about the placing of the organs in the body were taken as incontrovertible truth. When bodies were dissected, what was found did not accord with what Galen wrote: but it was always supposed that the observation must be erroneous, or the sample atypical, and Galen's authority remained supreme.

[13] It is worth noting that it was only from this time, or soon after, that writers in natural philosophy – what we call natural science – began to write in the dry, arid, prose that is now taken for granted in science. Before this time scientific observation was often lyrical, as in the following passage from the ancient Greek Empedocles:

When a girl, playing with a water-clock of shinning brass, puts the orifice of the pipe upon her comely hand, and dips the water-clock into the yielding mass of silvery water, the stream does not then flow into the vessel, but the bulk of the air inside, pressing upon the close-packed perforations, keeps it out till she uncovers the compressed stream; but then air escapes and an equal volume of water runs in.

Alternatively, scientific works were in narrative form, describing the successive attempts of the author to discover some phenomenon. If you have searched vainly through the *Accounting Review* or *Journal of Accounting Research* for any sign of style or wit, now you know whom to blame.

sin as a way of justifying his position: and it is in this way that the development parallels the developments in scientific thought.

However, although Bacon and Locke were prepared to break with the ecclesiastical traditionalists, we must not suppose that they were typical of their age. Breaking with centuries of tradition made them iconoclasts, and Hobbes in particular was attacked as a man of great wickedness for proposing what most economists and accounting theorists today take for granted. To take the individual's needs as a starting point, in other words, was *not* "obvious" or "common sense".

More important for our purposes than Bacon or Hobbes was John Locke (1632–1704). Locke's political philosophy, as we have already noted, is the foundation for modern democratic liberalism. Like Hobbes, he began with the notion of man in a state of nature. In this state man is free, and all men are equal. People in this state of nature have natural rights, notably rights to life, to liberty and to property in what they produce (those familiar with the clarion call in the US constitution will find the first two of these strike a familiar chord). However, Locke argued that such a state of nature was not practicable, because men's actions would conflict: hence men joined together into States. In these States, the duty of the ruler was to provide the conditions under which citizens might enjoy their rights. Should the ruler fail to do this, then they might remove him. With the exception of the natural rights, which were inalienable, there should be a democratic vote, with the majority view prevailing.

Especially interesting to us is that part of Locke's system that deals with property rights. Although in the natural state no one should have more than their basic living required, once men had come together in society, they had the right to accumulate property. They were to do so as free individuals, on merit as a result of industriousness, not as the result of what Samuel Beer calls the "old Tory" conception of a society ordered in rank by God, in which each person had their allotted place.

Locke's approach to knowledge, as we saw earlier, was empirical. That is, it did not admit of any knowledge prior to the sense data that comes to us from the world. To the empiricist, knowledge is based on experience. This is absolute: at birth the mind is, as Locke put it, "white paper, void of all characters". (Popper was later to use a less complimentary metaphor, referring to this as the "bucket theory of knowledge": it treats the human being as just a bucket into which knowledge is poured. Perhaps this tells us more about Popper than about Locke.) There are no innate ideas, said Locke. As a result, we have no basis for believing anything, except insofar as it can be the result of input from our senses. To the modern reader, coached in the language of computers, this appears to be analogous to suggesting that we have no explicit program to organize the data fed in to us, but that we have a sufficiently high processing power to sort out that data and eventually make sense of it.

Put this way, the empiricist's conclusion may seem odd. However, to some the alternative was to see knowledge as essentially innate, so that the foundation of our knowledge is prior to any experience at all: that is, we can know things of which we have no experience. Although clearly this raises questions about what we mean by "know", it is nevertheless a coherent and opposed opinion to empiricism. We shall meet it in more detail in Chapter 3.

Through the conduit of first Hume (1711–76), and later the positivism of the sociologist Comte and his successors, the empiricism of Hobbes and Locke leads us to the modern accounting reliance on empirical evidence, which has reached the stage where some leading journals are no longer prepared to publish any research unless it performs statistical tests on large data sets. The clear implication is that the only knowledge fit to be published is that which is culled from the empirical world.[14] Hume (1748), indeed, went further than Locke. In a famous passage he showed himself the forerunner of logical positivism:

> If we take in our hand any volume; of divinity or school metaphysics for instance, let us ask; *Does it contain any abstract reasoning concerning quantity or number?* No. *Does it contain any experimental reasoning concerning matter of fact and existence?* No. Commit it then to the flames: for it can contain nothing but sophistry and confusion.
> (*An Enquiry concerning Human Understanding*, Selby-Bigge, p. 165)

This is generally known as "Hume's fork". It appears to state that there are only two kinds of knowledge that may be taken as meaningful: one is deductive knowledge; the other is knowledge arising from empirical research. Nothing else, we are told, can count as knowledge. This in itself may seem to make the traditional accounting theorist very happy, since it appears to insist on the importance of thorough empiricism so as to increase

---

[14] Although some would argue that much of the direction of development of accounting theory has followed cognate developments in economics, it remains a fact that economic theorists, like theoretical physicists, command far greater respect (and win more Nobel Prizes) than econometricians or experimental physicists. In this respect, at least, accounting has not followed economics.

our store of knowledge. In fact, in Hume's sceptical hands, it does nothing of the kind. Hume investigates further the nature of our knowledge of the external world; and he effectively kills off any reason to have faith in developing useful models through what is now believed to be good scientific (that is, empirical) method (although, as we shall see later, there have been many suggested means of avoiding the worst problems identified by Hume). The problem arises because, in investigating the empirical world, we wish to develop the notion of *cause*.

To illustrate this, let us take a piece of HIPS research: in this case, Ashton's (1976) study on functional fixation. Ashton asked his subjects to make a product pricing decision: he then told them an accounting change had occurred and they were given new data. This should have resulted in decision changes, but many subjects continued to use the previous information base.

Now it may be that Ashton only wishes us to draw the conclusion that, on the particular occasion when he conducted his experiment, functional fixation occurred. This is unlikely. The result would then hardly be worth reporting, except as a curiosity. The experiment only gains its force because of its supposed generalized implications.

An alternative is to suppose that this may be expected to form an invariant pattern, so that it just so happens that when this situation occurs, there is functional fixation. But this is unlikely to be satisfactory, because we would then be offered no reason for supposing the coincidence of these phenomena next time. This leaves us with one final possibility: that we claim a causal relationship, where by "cause" we mean that (to keep the argument simple) *whenever* this kind of situation occurs we find functional fixation, because various intervening variables within the subjects' decision processes form a causal chain that leads to the phenomenon known as functional fixation. Hume is able to demonstrate that we can never prove causality (and indeed, any good statistics course is at pains to teach students as an elementary observation that, just because they have discovered a correlation, they have no grounds for supposing that they have demonstrated a causal relation). But Hume went further than this. We can *never* observe a causal relation, because that goes beyond the observable – a cause cannot present itself to our senses. One cannot hear or see a cause. As empiricists, we have already nailed our colours to the mast of the observable: that is, the empirical. As an empiricist, therefore, Hume effectively shows the poverty of the aspirations of empiricism. Within empiricism, we can never attain the objects for which we undertake empirical investigations.

CONCLUSION

The object of this chapter has been to outline the assumptions of the traditional paradigm in accounting. We have attempted to show that they cannot legitimately be "taken-for-granted" assumptions but must, like any other set of philosophical propositions, be defended against objections. Both as theory of society and theory of knowledge, they constitute the legacy of a mode of thought that had its genesis in the seventeenth century and which has been challenged vigorously by many thinkers since then. We have not attempted to outline by any means all of the features of empiricism; nor have we even scratched the surface of the challenges to empiricism. As the following chapters unfold, we shall see how many of the frameworks that form the basis for other approaches to accounting stem from those frameworks that are fundamentally opposed to the tenets of the individualistic and empiricist traditions. For now, we merely reiterate that traditional management accounting is as much the result of a set of theoretical philosophies as any other approach to understanding management accounting practices.

DISCUSSION QUESTIONS

1. If we take a technique like CVP analysis, can we claim it is empiricist because it claims to model real-world phenomena?
2. Find an academic paper that uses mathematical techniques to model management accounting processes. To what extent does it refer to the world of experience? Can it be truly criticized as being "empiricist", if it makes so little reference to the empirical world?
3. Is management accounting conceivable without property rights?
4. To what extent is "behavioural accounting" similar to, or different from, the techniques of the standard management accounting textbook?
5. Try to think of a value-free, unbiased statement within management accounting. Is your statement non-political?
6. We said above that traditional management accounting is rationalistic. Consider the following possibilities: (a) people's behaviour in organizations is not fully rational but management accounting is; (b) people's behaviour in organizations is rational and management accounting in practice reflects this; (c) neither people's behaviour nor management accounting

systems can be explained in terms of rationality. In answering this question, you may find it helpful to clarify what you mean by "rational".

7.   The last part of this chapter argued strongly that traditional management accounting does not rely on a "common sense" view of the world but is grounded in a particular philosophical school. Try to construct an argument to rebut this.

8.   We described positivism as being concerned with measurable phenomena that were perceivable by the senses. Think of some management accounting concepts (for example, profit, cost, variance, and overhead apportionment). Are these available to the senses? Are they real? If you conclude that the answer to the first question is "no", then (a) how is it that hard-headed businesspeople rely on them so much – or at least, talk about them so much? and (b) if they are not real, where "real" is defined as being available to the senses, then how do you distinguish them from fairies (which I am supposing are also not perceivable by the senses)?

2

Broadening Out: The Systems Perspective

INTRODUCTION

A key characteristic of traditional management accounting as we defined it in the previous chapter is that it is "reductionist". The key to understanding the systems approach is to realize that its foundations lie in attempting to overcome reductionism. This is true in both senses of the term. The systems approach breaks down barriers among traditional scientific disciplines. It also tries to view every problem as a whole, since it sees much of the essence of what is being considered in terms of its interconnectedness. This is summed up beautifully by a founder member of the systems movement, C. West Churchman. Churchman was criticizing the direction that operational research had taken since he had coauthored its first textbook, under the subheading "The dreary 60s".

During the 1960s in a large variety of departments, OR academically became "modelling", not really modelling at all, but a study of the delights of algorithms; nuances of game theory; fascinating but irrelevant things that can happen in queues ("a funny thing happened to me while I was waiting to cash a check"); expanding, involuting LP and non–LP – e.g. by decomposition. Even when "application" gets mentioned it is in terms of an article that never mentions implementation, or testing hypotheses. Meanwhile, the practice of

OR was presented to managers as "solving specific problems by models", exactly the opposite of our original intent. One of my colleagues at Berkeley, who practises in this manner, describes his method as "carving off a manageable problem". When he says this, I can't help visualizing a surgeon who says he needs to carve off a leg to see if he can get it working properly.

(Churchman, 1978, p. 3)

In its early days at any rate, this also became paradigmatic for taking the broader systems approach to accounting. To understand accounting, says the systems approach, we need to view it in its total organizational context (in contrast, for instance, to the individualistic behavioural budgeting literature that experiments with the individual through varying the task presented, abstracting it from any organizational context; this would be the equivalent of Churchman's surgeon).

Now to understand the workings of this broader, systems approach to understanding management accounting systems (much of the relevant literature tended to refer to an "organizational" approach, thus emphasizing the main system it investigated) we need to begin by looking at the systems approach itself. Only when we have some notion of its roots can we properly begin to appreciate its application to management accounting, and the way it is common or contrasting with other approaches in this book. We shall therefore begin with a discussion of the systems movement.

THE SYSTEMS MOVEMENT

There are often acknowledged to be two roots to the systems approach. One was the appearance of a seminal article by Ludwig von Bertalanffy called "The Theory of Open Systems in Physics and Biology" in 1950; the other was the formation of the Society for General Systems Research in 1954, one of the founder members being von Bertalanffy himself. The systems movement grew over the next twenty years or so, and may now be considered matured. It has, in a way, reached such a maturity that those who make use of its ideas, either explicitly or implicitly, may not be fully aware of the fundamental characteristics that distance them from other writers.

The philosophical roots of systems thinking

In the last chapter we saw that traditional theory might be understood through the history of ideas that formed the environment within which it flourished. In the same way, we can see the roots of systems ideas going back to well before this century. Some traces of thinking in holistic terms may be found in the works of the ancient Greeks. Anaximander and Thales, for example, sought for fundamental substance so as to demonstrate the essential unity of the world. Heraclitus emphasized change and movement in nature. None of this was surprising, since the search for an understanding of the *whole* world was axiomatic to the enquiries of the Greeks. However, its direct influence on systems thinking is probably negligible.

More important for our purposes is the nineteenth century philosopher Hegel, whose ideas were used by Churchman explicitly in, for example, his work on designing enquiring systems. Unfortunately, Hegel is among the most difficult of philosophers, and any attempt to interpret his work here would be presumptuous and misleading. We shall say here therefore only that two features of his work are significant for the systems approach. The first is his emphasis on the essential unity of the world (through something he called "spirit"). He argued that if anything less than the whole were to be contemplated, this would lead to contradictions, because the only truth lay in the whole, so that partial features wrenched out of the whole must be (in a way) false. The second is his dialectic, which through a continual questioning was equally founded in the connectedness of the world, both spatially and temporally. The dialectic is triadic. As adopted in the systems approach, it begins with the examination of a propostion – thesis; this is then found to contain contradictions, which lead to an antithesis; and finally the juxtaposition and resolution of these leads to a synthesis. This second may therefore be seen as a system of enquiry which is doubly systemic: both because it enquires into systems and because its own form is itself a system.

Now it may be that many of the early systems theorists had little formalized knowledge of philosophy. Yet both Churchman and Ackoff studied under the minor US philosopher Singer; Kenneth Boulding, as an economist trained at a great university in the early 1940s, would have been familiar with philosophical concepts; and Stafford Beer, a key systems theorist and cybernetician, also explicitly studied philosophy at the undergraduate level.

It would therefore be wrong to suppose they were only unconsciously influenced by past thinkers.

However, we are already running into difficulties. When we write of "the systems movement", we imply a singularity of approach among systems theorists. This would be misleading. There has been a great diversity, ranging from cybernetics, to the mathematical theory of fuzzy sets, to open systems theory. We shall make one key distinction here, between those who work within *general* systems theory, and those in *open* systems theory. The distinction between these will become clearer presently.

The tenets of the systems approach – general systems theory

The need for a systems approach was felt necessary because of a tendency in empirical science towards the analytical. First, the totality of science[1] has been divided among disciplines: physics, mathematics, chemistry, biology, psychology, and so on. Each of these is then further subdivided; thus we have organic and inorganic chemistry, social psychology and cognitive psychology, urban sociology and the sociology of religion. Frequently these break down into further specialisms. What is more, the method that is used for investigation tends to be analytic rather than synthetic. One of the great triumphs of science is said to be Mendelian genetics: and this progressed because Mendel studied one species of plant over many generations, isolating key characteristics, and repeating observations over and over again. Particle physics mostly progresses by isolating particles in an accelerator, keeping out all complicating phenomena. Skinnerian psychology advanced by reducing the variables to a pigeon and a stimulus. This has come to be known as *the* scientific model, to be emulated by all true scientists who thirst after knowledge.

While not denying the great progress made through these methods, systems theorists nevertheless ask if something does not eventually get missed through these methods. Let us take one simple example. The Stedry study was an award-winning example

---

[1] The term "science" is a curious one in the English language. It seems to have attracted around it a matrix of meanings. If a method is said to be scientific, we suppose it is methodical, moving through valid logic from premiss through hypothesis to experiment, and hence to conclusion. What is more, to most people it conjures illusions of white coats: it is physical science that is meant. Here we use the term more broadly, similarly to the German term *Wissenschaft*, to mean an organized body of knowledge.

of budgeting research. It was a laboratory study that gave (non-industrial) tasks to students, rewards for the attainment of "budgets", and tested various situations such as asking/not asking for an aspiration level; setting budgets of different levels of difficulty; and quantifying the resulting levels of performance. In this way it was a classical empirical study, with a dependent variable, a set of independent variables, and a hypothesized causal relation. The results were believed to be quite significant.[2] However, a systems theorist would plausibly argue that in the real world of the office or factory, by the time other variables had come into play (such as the budgetee's tiredness, the corporate culture, the stage of the budget cycle, previous experience of this and other budget systems, and the subject's personality) the Stedry variables would quite possibly shrink into insignificance in comparison to these other variables. To summarize the point briefly: the classical scientific model would have failed us completely in understanding the budget system in the real-world context.

To say this is not to know how to proceed in making sense of the complexity of systems. Some are simple, some are very complex. We can show how complex apparently simple systems are by taking an example of Stafford Beer's. Suppose we have a system that consists of an array of 100 light bulbs. Each bulb can be either on or off. How many states can the system take on? The system certainly seems straightforward: yet the answer is 2^{100}, which is about 1,260,000,000,000,000,000,000,000,000,000. This makes it a pretty complex system. Yet it is simplicity itself when compared to a company of 100,000 people, offices, factories, plant, each of which can take on a whole series of states. Clearly an organizing principle is needed to make sense of different kinds of system. A helpful approach is a classification scheme first suggested by Kenneth Boulding. On the face of it, the scheme may seem trite; and it does not make any claims that are susceptible to particular use: nevertheless it is a succinct synoptic

---

[2] This term can be a dangerous one. Statisticians use it quite differently from the use in everyday speech: there is a tendency to think that because a result is statistically significant it is therefore important. This is not so. For example, suppose we perform a multiple regression with twenty independent variables. One independent variable only constitutes 2 per cent of the variation of the dependent variable, but a t-test at a 0.001 level of significance shows we can be almost certain the relationship is genuine. The statistician would say the variable is significant, but to the world of cause and effect it is of very little importance compared to some of the other variables.

framework that is intuitively appealing as a way of approaching systems.

Boulding suggested that there were nine levels of system, from the simplest to the most complex. He described them as follows.

1. At the first and simplest level we have statics. These are systems that *as we define them* consist of no obvious movements or changes. The table at which I am sitting would be an example. So would a classification scheme itself, since it has no internal dynamic features.
2. At the second level are what he calls "clockworks": systems that move within given parameters. The planets are an example; so is a refrigerator. Although dynamic, these systems have no checking mechanism to ensure they work correctly: that is left to the third level of system.
3. The third level has a goal, and a means of testing whether that goal is being achieved. An example might be an industrial quality control system.
4. There is a sharp break to the fourth level. Here the system is open to the environment. The system has goal-seeking properties but, in addition, can check whether these have been fulfilled and, within limits, adjust its structures or even its goals when they are not fulfilled. Fourth-level systems are open: their essential nature includes the import and export of energy and information to and from the environment.

Now the attentive reader may object that the other systems we have described are also open: for instance a quality control system is open in the sense that new people come to work in it, from its environment. But it is not open in terms of its operational parameters and the information it handles. Thus we define openness in terms of the nature of the system itself.

The higher levels that Boulding then includes go through increasing levels of complexity in the plant, animal and human worlds, ending with, at the eighth level, human organizations (his ninth level he reserved for what he called "transcendental" systems, in which, among other things, he left space for systems of a complexity he could currently not conceive. These are not relevant to our present purpose). It is with the eighth level (and to a lesser extent the previous level – that of human beings) that we are especially concerned. Accounting systems operate within organizations. If we are to understand the implications of using a theoretical framework that is explicitly systems oriented, we need to know the theoretical basis that underpins the systems theory of organizations: and this is, in essence, open systems theory.

Open systems theory

The applications of systems ideas to organizations flourished during the 1960s. It drew not only from general systems theory, but also from the functionalist sociology of Talcott Parsons and others, which was then dominant in mainstream US sociology (we explained functionalism in Chapter 1). These sociologists had also conceived of societies as systems, and the ideas that crystallized in representing the nature of organizations as systems paralleled similar frameworks intended to represent the nature of social systems.

The characteristics of open systems listed below are culled from Katz and Kahn (1966) and Litterer (1969).

Systems are holistic

This means that the whole is greater than the sum of its parts: in contrast to reductionism, holism recognizes that only through looking at the totality of an organization might it be understood. Given that systems consist of elements and relationships between elements, holism places the relationships on an equal footing with the elements themselves. This matters, because things interact. As Ashby (1955) drily put it, one penny combined with one penny gives you two pennies, because the pennies do not interact. Contrast this, he says, with one rabbit and another rabbit. "Here there is real interaction, and the outcome cannot be represented as a simple sum".

Systems are characterized by input, transformation and output

They take in energy from their environments, transform it in some way, and return it back to the environment in its transformed state. Besides including the obvious types of energy (such as sunshine into agricultural organizations and electricity into manufacturing industry) this also includes raw materials and the labour of the people concerned in the organization. You will probably recognize the "input" here as being similar to the economist's "factors of production".

Organizational systems exhibit teleology

They have a purpose, and are generally designed to pursue that purpose, with mechanisms to recognize when that purpose is or is not being fulfilled. Mostly they also contain elements to change the purpose itself when this is deemed desirable, fruitful and/or feasible. They are self-regulatory, and are able to make quite complex adjustments to themselves in order to ensure that they are kept "on course". This may be a simple negative feedback (such as a budget variance that results in an adjustment to a production process). In contrast, it may be a learning process, whereby the organization discovers that some aspects of its actual structure or operations or goals are inappropriate, and takes action to modify them. This is best understood by contrasting the regulated organization with the equally regulated thermostatically controlled room, a far simpler regulator. The thermostat can recognize when a room is too cold, and can turn on a heater. It cannot recognize that the windows need extra insulation and carry this out, however. Nor can it recognize the wearing-out of its own parts. The eighth-level organization is able to achieve the equivalent of both of these.

Open systems are negentropic

Entropy, a concept borrowed from thermodynamics, describes the tendency of any system such that, over time, its elements will move to a state of maximum probability and minimal differentiation. A steel bar if heated at one end, for example, will begin with one end being hotter than the other. However, if left in a vacuum it will, over time, alter its state so that the temperature is uniform throughout. Open systems exhibit tendencies to negative entropy: they have characteristics that help them in preventing this "running down".[3] One such characteristic is differentiation. After a long period, no part of our steel bar could be distinguished by its temperature from any other: difference has vanished. Organizations exhibit significant differences (for instance, some parts are more adaptive to their environments;

---

[3] The tendency to entropy is so common that we take it for granted: you may even doubt there is a "real" principle here. If so, ask yourself the question: how likely is it that such a bar, left to itself in a vacuum, will spontaneously change in the *opposite* direction, with one end getting hotter and the other cooler? This is just what negative entropy entails: but you do not find it in simple closed systems.

some have higher labour intensity; some are in conflict with others). This helps sustain them through a richness, or variety, of possible adaptive responses to difficulties they face.

Open systems differentiation also takes the form of hierarchy

Just as the tree trunk is differentiated from the branch and the twig, so some parts of organizations tend to dominate and control others. Each part is a subsystem in its own right, and may tend to exhibit all the characteristics we have just described of total systems. The result of this is, of course, that we could model whole societies in a systems sense such that organizations are subsystems of societies, departments are subsystems of organizations, people are subsystems of departments, and so on.

Open systems are controlled through a mechanism of information input, negative feedback and coding

Besides the physical input of energy, systems receive information about the state of the environment and their own states.[4] One special input is the negative feedback that results from each system's own output and goals, so as to correct deviations. There is a massive amount of such information to process: open systems handle this potential complexity by have coding mechanisms so as to filter out information which is considered inessential (most organizations would filter out information as to who won a particular football match: however, this could be important information to an organization that was itself a football club). Through this feedback mechanism, then, organizations may achieve a steady state and dynamic homeostasis. A system in steady state is one that is relatively invariant in the relationships among its parts. In any three months, for example, the personnel, procedures and relationships within the marketing department of a company will change little, if at all. Yet all the time, work itself is flowing through. Thus "steady state" does not mean

---

[4] The importance of information to systems theory cannot be overemphasized. Organization can in fact be defined through information. Consider the discussion of entropy, above. A system of maximum entropy is undifferentiated: this means we cannot tell one part from another. Through the work of Shannon and Weaver, we define information through surprise. If we cannot tell one state from another state, there is zero information. Only through differentiation does information arise; and conversely, only through information can we tell that one part of a system is differentiated from another. Accounting systems are of course one key example of information systems generally.

"motionless". Homeostasis refers to the ability of an organism to adjust to environmental disturbances and survive, which it does through multiple regulators that sense changes in relevant variables, and react to counter or take advantage of them. Dynamic homeostasis refers to the fact that an organism may not just survive, but actually grow and prosper in the midst of such environmental disturbance.

It is here in particular that systems theory interacts with cybernetics. Cybernetics is concerned with steersmanship: with the control of the direction of an entity through feedback and learning mechanisms. Its principles have been used extensively in machine design; but organizational cyberneticians have been especially interested in the survival properties of living organisms. Stafford Beer expressed it like this:

> What aspects of biological control does the cybernetician find so impressive? Here is an informal list: natural organisms are self-regulatory, and self-organizing; they are adaptive to environmental and internal change; they learn from their own experience; they are robust, in that the failure of a component part does not seem to matter; and they seek solutions which favour overall advancement, not allowing parts of the system to develop local successes inimical to the success of the organic whole. In a word, biological controls conduce to survival.
>
> (Beer, 1962)

What does all this mean for "systems philosophy"?

So far, our list of systems characteristics has seemed a little arid – sometimes a statement of the obvious – and certainly has seemed little related to accounting systems. Before we turn to the way this approach has come to permeate sections of accounting thinking, therefore, we need to stand back and ask about the result of approaching problems in systems terms, and depicting the organizations whose accounting systems are analysed as systems that operate and can be understood through this framework.

The essential feature of most systems theory is *equilibrium*. Because all the systems and subsystems of a society contain regulatory mechanisms (homeostats), they tend to exhibit equilibrium in themselves, and in the relationships among themselves. This is a very powerful notion. Following, to some extent, from the functionalist paradigm in sociology and anthropology, we can conceive society and its constituent organizations as being in balance. They move from one state to another, but all the time are able to handle disturbances (which are themselves, by implication, dysfunctional) sufficiently well to minimize any harm from them. The picture is one of serenity: one in which the disturbance (which is external, because there is no place in this picture for any notion of inherent instabilities that are internal to the system) can always be nullified or adapted to.[5]

Systems theory is believed by many of its exponents to be value-neutral. Systems just are as they are: they exhibit the characteristics we have outlined, and a good scientist can explore and develop further ideas from these characteristics. However, this proposition is far from unchallengeable. By taking equilibrium as axiomatic, there is a tendency to perceive equilibrium where there may be none. Suppose, for example, that we observe a disruption to a production system caused by some external factor (a delay in supplies of raw materials) which is faithfully reported by the costing system. An equilibrating mechanism moves in to counter it (phoning around to find an alternative urgent supply).

On which event do we place the emphasis? Do we have an inherently and naturally unstable system, in which there is continual disruption, which homeostats temporarily succeed in neutralizing? Or do we take the opposite view, that the equilibrium is the natural state, and each particular disturbance is only a blip in an otherwise comfortable picture? This is not a trivial question of the nature, "Is this bottle half-full or half-empty?", because within the answer lies the basic nature of society, of its systems, of our human experience, and of the nature of the accounting systems and their relations to the organizations that they serve.

With this as a preliminary comment, we now turn to the way that the accounting literature has worked within a systems paradigm.

INFORMATION SYSTEMS AND ACCOUNTING SYSTEMS

When we turn to the accounting literature that is rooted in the systems paradigm, we find that it is, perhaps, less self-consciously aware of the nature of its own roots than any of the works that we shall discuss in the following three chapters. To a greater

---

[5] A rider is needed here. Tinker's early work was explicitly systems-oriented; however he treated equilibrial tendencies very differently, seeing social systems as inherently unstable, and the homeostatic tendencies of individual systems as just temporary coping mechanisms. See Lowe and Tinker, 1977, for example.

extent than with them, it has come to share with the traditional approach, perhaps because it is the nearest of the four to the traditional approach and relies the most heavily on "common sense", a disregard for its philosophical roots. It feels a correspondingly lesser need to interrogate those roots.

Now if you pick up a book from the library or bookshop that includes the word "system" in its title, there is a good chance that it will be a book on information systems and particularly, computerized information systems. Since the advent of the mainframe computer and its use by business organizations, there has been a profusion of discussion of the systematization of information provision. Before the centralized computer, individual departments tended to have their own sources of information; and they stored the information themselves. Once centralized data processing departments appeared, they tended to attempt to centralize the collection and dissemination of information.

Although the management information systems (MIS) literature has been extensive as one part of management control (and it may be argued that management accounting is just a subset of management information; cf. Earl, 1983), it has made few acknowledgements to general systems theory as a progenitor (cf., for example, Earl and Hopwood, 1980; Mitroff and Mason, 1983). A general characteristic of the early literature was an intense rationality, particularly in the textbooks (Hicks, 1984). Organizational systems were complex, they had to be managed: and a rational design was described to aid managers who, it was supposed, acted rationally as far as possible themselves. Later this began to break down. Hedberg and Jönsson's (1978) paper is well-known as suggesting that in some circumstances the provision of clear and unambiguous information was not necessarily desirable, given the tendency of information and organization systems to use filtering techniques to handle the proliferation of information enveloping the organization, and hence to create institutional barriers to information that might be disturbing and signal major changes in the environment. In fact the notion of ambiguity became increasingly common during the 1980s. Cooper, Hayes and Wolf (1981) used the ideas of Weick (1979) and March and Olsen (1976) to argue that organizations are contexts into which people pour problems, solutions, participants and choice opportunities. The system is not a "rational" one that follows a logical progression of {find problem → seek solution → find solution → implement solution}. Instead, March and Olsen put it like this:

Suppose we view a choice opportunity as a garbage can into which various problems and solutions are dumped by participants. The mix of garbage in a single can depends partly on the labels attached to the alternative cans; but it also depends on what garbage is being produced at the moment, on the mix of cans available, and on the speed with which garbage is collected and removed from the scene.

(Cooper *et al.*, 1981, p. 26)

So the whole system, in facing ambiguity in its organizational environment, abandons the "apparent-rational" model. This creates problems for accounting systems which,

by *what* they measure, *how* they measure and *who* they report to can effectively delimit the kind of issues addressed and the ways in which they are addressed. They reflect the status quo, the appropriate and acceptable ways of doing things and talking about issues.

(Cooper *et al.*, 1981, p. 182)

Though this may seem to be undermining the systems approach, it is in fact wholly consistent with it. We may interpret this subversion of the traditional accounting information system as simply a remapping of its methods so as to continue, like all good systemic information systems, to aid the system in survival. This is particularly clear in Dyckman's parallel discussion of the problems of ambiguity and choice; his paper ends by stating that "it behoves us to keep abreast of the developments in the understanding of behavior and to integrate these ideas into our teaching, our practice, and our applied research" (1981, p. 299). Even March's own (1987) insightful paper in the accounting literature, while suggesting that:

information engineering – like research, journalism and education – might well find part of its character grounded in theories of history, language, culture, art and criticism.

(March, 1987, p. 164)

is not suggesting anything radical, other than a heightened appreciation of the nature of information in the business organization. It is still, therefore, systems orientated.

THE ORGANIZATIONAL APPROACH TO ACCOUNTING SYSTEMS

Perhaps the most obvious use of systems ideas in accounting research has developed in contingency theories of accounting systems. These start from two notions. First, that there is the need for design, in this case, the most appropriate design for a management accounting control system as part of the organization's more general set of control systems. Second, there is the acknowledgment that, fundamental to this design there is the need to take into account the internal and external environments of the organization; and that different environmental characteristics will in all probability lead to different control system configurations.

This approach had a further progenitor, in addition to the general systems theory and functionalist social theory mentioned above. This was the contingency school of organizational design that grew from the early works of Woodward, Burns and Stalker, and of Lawrence and Lorsch (although these in turn were derived from the systems theory propositions we have just outlined). The contingency approach in organization theory was a reaction against scientific management and human relations approaches, both of which had prescribed universalistic rules for management. These rules, often by implication, were supposed to lead to good management, no matter what the organization or the circumstances.

By the time accounting theorists had begun to look outward beyond narrowly technical and psychological factors for their explanations and designs, organizational theorists had accumulated a substantial body of theoretical work and practical empirical research into contingency theories of organizational design. Accounting theory too was seeking an approach that no longer prescribed a universal set of rules to be followed when designing an accounting system. The factors that were perceived to be important to organizations included technological complexity, environmental dynamism and complexity, and organizational size.

This was extended into a contingency theory of accounting (cf., for example, Bruns and Waterhouse, 1975; Hayes, 1977; Gordon and Miller, 1976; Amigoni, 1978; Ginzberg, 1980; Markus and Pfeffer, 1983; Rockness and Shields, 1984; Gordon and Narayanan, 1984; Simons, 1987; and Williams, Macintosh and

Moore, 1990[6]). These and other studies are in essence systemic. Like traditional studies they conceive of their rationale not in any disinterested "scientific" mode, although their empirical method relies on statistical inference, but rather in terms of managerial problem-solving. Although this is not always explicit, frequently it is. Bruns and Waterhouse explicitly refer to "managerial implications" and "enhancing the effectiveness of budgetary control". In the 1990s this kind of explicit reference seems to be on the wane (similar examples are absent from the later works quoted above). On the other hand, there is no obvious reason to conduct most of this problem-centred research if it is not ultimately justified in terms of its practical usefulness. These texts do not, after all, make riveting reading, stylistically.

We now turn to a more detailed examination of some of these readings, not to discuss their substantive findings (a task more appropriate to a more conventional "advanced" management accounting text – see, for example, Emmanuel, Otley and Merchant, 1990; Ezzamel and Hart, 1987), but to examine their reliance on the systems concept.

Contingency models of accounting systems

An early attempt at a general contingency model was that of Gordon and Miller (1976). This begins with a systems diagram (see Figure 2.1). Pointing out that each of the four systems/factors can differ in its characteristics, the main part of the paper hypothesizes relationships between the states of the characteristics of each factor that will lead to effectiveness, claiming that "no one prescribed [accounting information] system could ever be effective in all circumstances". The paper has the flavour of many of the individual studies that were to follow it. The subsystems could be clearly identified; their characteristics could be enumerated; the states of the characteristics could be identified: and these would, in principle at least, be amenable to quantification, measurement, and statistical investigation. Through acknowledging the interaction among the features the programme is apparently holistic; and by incorporating a performance feature

---

[6] Otley (1980) begins his early analysis and critique of contingency studies in accounting with his own and Hopwood's studies of budget systems and behaviour. Frameworks shade into one another – the cut-off point between this chapter and the previous one is contestable. Those and similar studies are omitted, since they appear relatively unsystemic as systems are defined here.

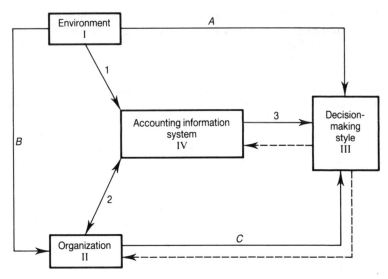

FIGURE 2.1

("effectiveness" in the quotation given above) an implicit purposiveness is ascribed to each organization analysed.

Interesting in this context, however, are the open systems
characteristics that the schema omits. We said it was holistic: yet
all the relationships posited are actually reductionist. Thus, to
return to Figure 2.1, the paper proposes expected relationships
between the environment and the accounting information system.
In doing so, it ignores the states of the organization (for example)
at that time. To make this clearer, suppose each of the three (I,
II and IV) could take on only two states, $\{E_1, E_2\}$; $\{AIS_1, AIS_2\}$;
$\{O_1, O_2\}$. Now suppose we hypothesize a relationship between
the environmental states and AIS such that we expect a mapping
$\xi = \{E_1 \leftrightarrow AIS_1, E_2 \leftrightarrow AIS_2\}$. In so doing it assumes the mapping
ξ is the same whether the organization is in state O_1 or O_2. It
should be immediately clear that this is not consistent with
systems theory, which acknowledges the potential saliency of all
variables (remember the 100 light bulbs earlier?).

A second way that this kind of schema transgresses systems
theory is by omitting any possibility of equifinality. The hypothesis
is that a single mapping should be found that will be effective.
Yet equifinality proposes that self-organizing systems may find
many ways of being successful. For instance, suppose we extend
the above example so that there are ten possible states of each of

the three variables. Then we may find that $\{E_1 \leftrightarrow AIS_3\}$ is successful when O is in state O_2, but that $\{E_1 \leftrightarrow AIS_8\}$ is successful when O is at state O_7. We may go further: this is the whole point of organizational design and learning mechanisms. Were it not so, design would be simple: but it is not.

These comments may appear to suggest that the analysis is not a "true" systems analysis. Certainly the model does not conform with the black box protocols suggested by Ashby and others.[7] Yet it undoubtedly is a systems model. It is concerned with the behaviour of teleological systems open to their environments that transform inputs into outputs, with internal and external complexity and learning through feedback (otherwise how are we to suppose the AIS came to be what it is?).

A second synoptic contingency model was the one proposed by Flamholz, Das and Tsui (1985). Their model is shown in Figure 2.2. However their introductory comments contrast sharply with Gordon and Miller. The language of systems theory is more explicit:

> Our view of control assumes that organizations and individuals are purposeful, goal-seeking entities, whose goals may not be congruent . . . Goal congruence is conceived to be a more powerful theoretical foundation for organizational effectiveness than action or outcome congruence because of the systems characteristic of equifinality . . . This new framework espouses a concept of control that is cybernetic in nature and also accommodates an open systems view of the organization and its environment.
>
> (pp. 36, 37)

The Flamholz *et al.* study has a second systems characteristic missing from Gordon and Miller: it is overtly interdisciplinary, explicitly drawing from organizational psychology, sociology and administrative theory. Curiously, it disclaims Stafford Beer's cybernetics, while starting its modelling from the planning-

---

[7] A black box is a system about which we have to assume nothing is known. We then attempt to find the behaviour of the whole box (system) by changing various input variables and logging what happens to the output variables. The series of different inputs is referred to as a protocol. In principle, if we continue experimenting with the input variables long enough, we can discover the whole set of functional relationships that the system controls. Indeed, if a box is *truly* black, this is the only way to understand its behaviour.

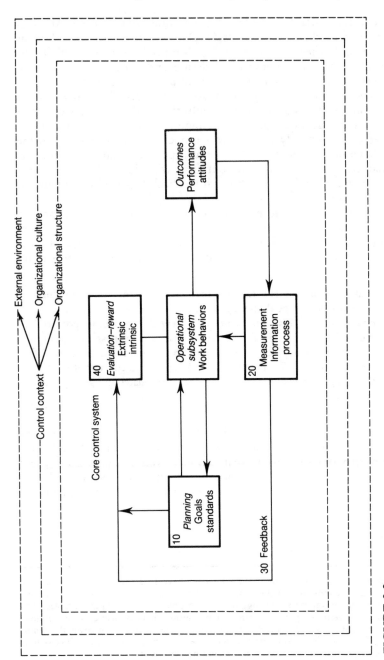

FIGURE 2.2

measuring-feedback framework which it correctly describes as cybernetic.[8]

These two suggested integrative frameworks are fairly successful examples of using systems concepts to understand organizational control. When we come to the individual contingency studies, the problems we discussed concerning Gordon and Miller's reductionism come to the fore. Basically, although appearing to be organizational rather than individually psychologistic, the perceived need in these studies for reliable quantification of variables and their relationships results in most cases in reductionism. Thus Bruns and Waterhouse (1975) consider just two variables: organization structure (albeit a variety of features of structure) and budget systems. Hayes (1977), considering departmental performance, looked at internal factors, environmental factors, and factors concerned with the interrelationship between departments. Rockness and Shields (1984) related the importance of controls to contextual variables and found this factor to be associated with technological uncertainty, but not with three other task-related factors. Gordon and Narayanan (1984) suggested from their study that the AIS and organization structure were both functionally related to the environment. Interestingly they found that after controlling for the environment, there was no significant relationship between the AIS and the organization's structure (this latter point relates to our "black box" criticism of Gordon and Miller and others earlier for a lack of systems method in an essentially system study). More recently, Williams, Macintosh and Moore (1990) have looked at the way that budget-related behaviour relates to performance, it being contingent on the extent of task interdependency.

A more recent innovation is the intervention of strategy as a variable (Simons, 1987). Simons studies the relationship between the firm's AIS and its strategy in the context of its performance.

With the slight exception of Simons' work, these studies do not mention systems theory at all (though Simons references Ashby's principle of requisite variety). It is, perhaps, now part of the taken-for-granted of contingency research programmes. Referring back to Chapter 1, we find that they take for granted the propriety of taking a uniquely managerial viewpoint; they suppose that entities exist "out there" unaffected by the research

---

[8] In disclaiming Beer's influence it may be referring to the Ashbian formulations of requisite variety and similar concepts that permeate Beer's seminal book. This would be correct: their model does indeed omit these features. It might be argued that this is one of their model's chief lacunae.

itself; that the important variables can be measured and that statistical techniques will uncover any relationships that exist. The research is ahistorical, since only cross-sectional variables from questionnaires are included in the models and therefore, by implication, historical factors are of relatively little import; it is rationalistic because it supposes that the systems uncovered are either deliberately designed in the way they operate so as to achieve a purpose, or else that they developed over time through a process of Darwinian attrition: and that it is purportedly value-free and apolitical (since nothing remotely political is ever mentioned).

Above all, these studies are founded on quantification. Only reified variables can be quantified. It is supposed unquestioningly, therefore, that there are phenomena to be studied; that those phenomena can be completely captured through quantifying and measuring their visible behaviour; and that any resulting indications of statistical association among the measured quantities are informative about the underlying phenomena themselves.[9]

CONCLUSION

In this chapter we have examined the nature of systems theory and its expression through various management accounting studies. These are enriched when compared to traditional studies, since they acknowledge the insights that come from interdisciplinary study, and they acknowledge the significance of complexity in the interrelations among the various parts of organizations. They are, however, expressly managerial in their orientation. Beginning with the next chapter, that managerial viewpoint starts to dissolve.

DISCUSSION QUESTIONS

1. Explain what is meant by (a) holism, (b) homeostasis, (c) equifinality, (d) coding, (e) negentropy. If you are considering this question as a member of a discussion group, which is of course a system itself, explain/give examples of each of them in terms of that discussion group.

---

[9] A well-known and more extensive critique of contingency approaches appeared many years before many of the studies mentioned here – see Otley, 1980.

2. What do we mean if we say a management accounting system should "fit" its environment?
3. "All real-life management accounting systems *must* fit their environments. If they did not, they would not last so long that we could observe them. So if they survive, this shows they are fine." Do you agree?
4. Explain the mutual adaptation of an organization and its management accounting system through time in terms of dynamic homeostasis.
5. Why do we describe an organization as an "open" system? Is a management accounting system open in this sense?
6. Based on traditional management accounting textbooks, do you see management information systems and management accounting systems as separate, or the latter as a subset of the former?
7. Go back to our discussion of relations among elements (with Ashby's reference to pennies and rabbits). Give examples of the way in which these interrelationships among departments can be significant for the budgetary reporting systems of particular departments in a business organization.
8. To what extent would you agree with the claim that systems/contingency models for management accounting can only be meaningful through their implications for the better design of management accounting systems?

3

Closing In: Stories From Microsociology

The kind of philosophy one chooses depends upon what sort of person he is. A philosophical system is not a lifeless collection of odds and ends that could be discarded or retained at whim. It is animated, rather, by the soul of the man who holds it.

– Fichte

In the last chapter we looked at systems theory. In what it was trying to achieve, this was not fundamentally different from traditional approaches to management accounting. Like traditional management accounting, systems theory was about making things work better within the status quo. It was concerned with understanding and prediction in order to effect control. It revolved around the proposition that if, through understanding objects as systems, we can predict better what is happening and what is likely to happen (because we have succeeded in effecting closure to the system), then we shall be able to control and sustain our system. Since systems are recursive, this is an all-embracing intent. The systems approach observes that we have troubles in all levels of system, from the level of society as a whole down to the level of the individual; and if we can only understand how these systems operate, then its tenets are believed to offer a means of improving each of these different levels of system.

That control perspective and intention is, in general, *not* continued into the interactionist perspective[1] considered in this chapter (although some think the ideas outlined here can be used that way). The motivation behind interactionist analysis is, certainly, to understand: but it is not an instrumentalist understanding that conceives of research as being a social maintenance job. Interactionists are not social engineers. They do not begin their task with the intention of creating smoother running systems: indeed, most interactionists would deny that the notion of system is a useful or even a meaningful one in social analysis.

Systems theory, as we have seen, is concerned with understanding so as to be able to take action. However, it does not recognize any problems inherent in the perception of the situation. Problems are "out there": the researcher's task is to comprehend the nature of those problems. The problems that face those who espouse systems theory lie, in particular, in the physical and organizational complexity of the object(s) examined. However demanding it may be, the systems approach supposes that there is a single reality to be understood, and that if only the tools were available, that understanding would in principle be possible (although much of the work of cybernetics in particular has revolved around the acknowledgement that, in practice, protocols are necessary to get working models of systems because of the very complexity of those systems). Thus the difficulties acknowledged by the systems theorist are problems of information: but a major difficulty acknowledged by action theorists is the problem of interpretation.

In now turning to interactionism, we are concerned with problems of understanding that are restricted to *people*. Systems theory was designed to apply equally to systems of things (machines) and to systems of people (social systems) and to the relationships between them (such as the socio-technical systems approach of organizational analysis pioneered by Trist and Bamforth). Interactionism, as its name suggests, is concerned particularly with the interaction among people in social situations: and the key lies in the interactionist's belief that understanding human behaviour is in its very nature different from understanding physical phenomena. We shall consider the reasons for this belief

---

[1] I use the term interactionist here; in other places I use "action theory". Because we are considering a number of differentiated but broadly similar approaches from sociology here, the terms are not agreed. We shall continue to use these fairly interchangeably.

presently. To begin with we turn to the historical roots of interactionism in interpretation studies.

THE HERMENEUTIC ROOTS OF INTERACTIONISM

Historically, the roots of the various interactionist approaches are to be found in the rise of hermeneutics towards the end of the eighteenth century in Germany (although this in turn may be traced back to philosophical idealism and the Kantian turn: that is, the schools of thought basically opposed to empiricism as a foundation for knowledge). Hermeneutics is concerned with understanding, which is often left in its German form, *Verstehen*. This movement grew through the problem of understanding texts – in particular, biblical texts.

The doctrine of the Catholic Church, which was the only Western church until the Reformation, was, and is, that there are two sources of our knowledge of the spiritual. One is the Bible. The other is the tradition of the Church. The Protestants challenged this: having turned away from the Catholic Church's authority, they denied its saliency and, in doing so, proposed the Bible as the sole authority for the word of God. At first it was argued that this need not be mediated by any other body of knowledge such as tradition. The Word spoke for itself. But there were clear difficulties with this belief, especially once the Bible had been translated into the vernacular (and indeed, before that the Bible had been available in Latin, which was not the source language of the Bible, either).

These biblical foundations are important, since the Bible was acknowledged to be the word of God. Hence the meaning of the text was of paramount importance. A means was needed to make sense of texts in such a way that the intentions of the author could be made manifest. There was a maxim among those making sense of divine texts: *sensus non est inferendus, sed eferendus* (meaning must be read out of, not into the text). An unbreakable cord was taken for granted that linked author to text. The text was the word of the author. This meant that, as the propositions of textual exegesis were developed and applied to texts beyond the Bible, they were seen as a means to understand better what the author had intended. This could best be done, according to the philologists Ast and Ast, by entering into the "spirit of antiquity".[2] One could only make sense of difficult passages by immersion into this spirit, as a result of which the passage could be understood in its fullest context and, hence, its meaning be revealed. Only when you knew what it *felt like* to be in ancient times could you really claim to understand a text written in those times.

In the years following, there were a number of influential German writers developing the ideas of hermeneutics. At this stage the task was still conceived as being to understand the real or essential meaning of the text. This in turn meant understanding the intentions of the author as fully as possible – as the author wished them to be understood. Hermeneutics was most fully developed by, and taken to its extreme in the work of Schleiermacher in the first half of the nineteenth century, who contended that hermeneutics should seek to understand the author better than the author himself or herself. However, the apotheosis of hermeneutics came, perhaps, with Wilhelm Dilthey, who began the process of extending the scope of hermeneutics beyond that of understanding the textual author to that of understanding cultures and societies, since culture was now regarded as the key to unlocking the meaning of the author's words.

It is not necessary here to trace Dilthey's work, but we shall briefly mention two difficulties that were faced by hermeneutics. The first of these is the hermeneutic circle; the second is a kind of "problem of empathy".

The hermeneutic circle was expressed by Dilthey like this:

> The totality of a work must be understood through its individual propositions and their relations, and yet the full understanding of an individual component presupposes an understanding of the whole.
>
> Dilthey, *Gesammelte Schriften*, Vol. VII, p. 225

The hermeneutic circle can begin to look like a vicious circle: because if A can only be understood through B (where B is a superset of A) and yet B can only be understood through A and its fellow propositions, how can we proceed? This problem exercised Dilthey, and led to a complex web of propositions that we cannot enter into here.

Turning to the second difficulty to which we referred, we note that, following from Ast and Ast, we need to, in a way, "put ourselves in the shoes" of the person or institution we are seeking

---

[2] Much of the argument of these paragraphs is based on Outhwaite, 1975.

to understand.[3] Can I understand Napoleon if I am not Napoleon, or if I have never led an army? Indeed, even if I have led an army, can I understand Napoleon, for I am still not Napoleon? And if not, how can I hope to "understand"?

This can be framed in the context of the accounting situation. Suppose I am a researcher trying to understand the negotiation of a budget in a chemical company that is facing a declining market for its product. The people involved are the managers and the chief accountant. Can I hope to understand what is happening in this negotiation if I have never been a chief accountant in a declining chemical company? And even (unlikely as it might be) if I have held this position in the past, I would still have no grounds for understanding the managers in the current negotiation. It would be just too difficult for me to "put myself in their place". Indeed, since each situation is unique (if only because this particular negotiation must be taking place in a different plant and at a different time from when I received my own relevant experience) even if I had had that experience, it would still not help me to *fully* understand what is happening. Worse still, if I did manage to write a research report on what I found, any reader of my report will face the same problem in making sense of my text: because he or she will have been neither me nor (almost certainly) a chemical company manager or chief accountant. The method therefore relies on the fact that, as a researcher, I am a person, and like the person who is a chief accountant in a chemical company, I take action in the face of the world given my understanding of it. But this may not be enough.

These then, are the kinds of difficulty facing *Verstehen*. They might seem insuperable, and put this way perhaps they are. Yet this does not obviate the seeming need for understanding. To say something is difficult is not to say it should not be attempted, especially if the alternatives seem decidedly less insightful. To appreciate this we need to consider the converse way of approaching a problem, through positive empiricist methods: in other words, through using the methods of the natural sciences.

---

[3] This of course emphasizes and exemplifies the difference between natural science and hermeneutics. It would be a nonsense to think of putting myself in the shoes of an atom of hydrogen, to see under what conditions I might "decide" to combine with another atom to produce a molecule.

HOW DO INTERPRETIVE STUDIES DIFFER FROM POSITIVIST STUDIES?

Interpretive studies contend that we can only make sense of the social world through an understanding of people *as* people. This means that any research study can only proceed through an understanding of how people understand each other's behaviour, rather than through some "objective" account, on the part of the researcher, into what happened.

One common distinction here is between behaviour and action (although this linguistic distinction is not followed by all authors). "Behaviour" refers to physical and non-human phenomena. Gases when heated behave in a certain way. Polymers under given situations behave in predictable ways. So do atoms, and planets. But people are different, not just because there is more variety in their responses to situations and to stimuli (in statistical terms, because there is a higher variance in their predicted behaviour when considered as a random variable) but rather because the nature of the person is different. People *act*. This action is *intentional*. People act so as to achieve goals,[4] rather than causally, as a (more or less determined) result of stimuli. If they did they would be relays, not people. Action is the result of an understanding. When a person acts it is not because a situation is as it is, but because they *perceive and believe* a situation to be as it is. We shall expand on this point shortly. This means too that there are potential problems in treating people as wholly consistent and rational, where rationality implies an invariant and hence predictable response to a particular stimulus under a given set of circumstances, and in accordance with a set of criteria (which is the approach taken by most brands of economics).

The result is an alternative to positivist empiricism, and particularly to its *method*: the belief that you can apply the methods of the natural sciences to social science and obtain a meaningful result. Although clearly the methods of the physical sciences include quantification (most interactionist research shows no interest in quantification), they include much more besides. One such feature is that positivism (the term we shall use for the methods of the physical sciences) requires that there should be simplification: we cannot handle the whole in its complexity (you

---

[4] This is not as simple a matter as it seems from this ingenuous statement. There are a number of objections to the idea that we perceive a goal before us and then act to achieve that goal. You will recognize that this implies a rationality that is far from universal in human activity.

are reminded of Churchman's admonition in Chapter 2). But in simplifying, we inevitably lose something.

What is perhaps paradoxical is that the positivist method which asks that situations be simplified for the sake of understanding also requires that the results be replicable. If this could be done (and interactionists deny that it can) then the method of simplification would also have to be the same. But this is a violence to method: a straitjacket that results in some of the complexities *never* being researchable because, by definition, that would then lead to a result that would not replicate a previous result. By replication I mean of course that, if a scientific experiment is undertaken under a given set of conditions and then repeated keeping the conditions the same, the outcome should always also be the same.[5]

As Colville (1981) has pointed out in discussing Glaser and Strauss's mistrust of *a priori* theorizing (as opposed to allowing the theory to develop from the observation itself), such theorizing harks back to positivism; and it has to require some notion of evidence that can confirm or disconfirm the theory. But to take this approach is to acknowledge the objectivity of the situation. That is also denied by interpretive approaches. Theory testing requires some objectivity. It also requires replicability. Neither is possible in the case of the social situation, because each situation is unique. Interestingly, this also leads to the conclusion that the researcher is asking us to trust him or her: the researcher's understanding and theory become paramount. The theory must come from the researcher; and it follows that since the situation considered will never be repeated, we have to trust the researcher's reading of the situation. There is no chance of replicating and thus confirming the results. This, its opponents would argue, is a major defect of the approach: yet the strength of the approach also lies in this, for the uniqueness of the situation is necessarily recognized. No uniformity is forced on to the situation, whereby

---

[5] Those with some knowledge of quantum mechanics will recognize that this simple picture does not apply at the quantum level. Indeed, the writings of major scientists who, unlike positivist accounting theorists, understand the nature of quantum theory and the significance of the observer can frequently sound remarkably like the social scientist discussing the importance of the individual researcher in making sense of the individual social situation. However, it is dangerous and naïve to draw too strong an inference from this. One might accuse those working within a naturalistic paradigm in accounting research of seeking the respectability of "real science" by emulating its methods. To seek succour for alternative paradigms while still clinging to the respectability of "real but different science" is to fall into the same trap.

one might look for a "class of situations" of its kind, and then use the observation to predict the course of future events in "such situations". Instead, what is unique to the situation is recognized as such: this strengthens the significance of the interpretation.[6]

There is another feature of positivism that contrasts strongly with interpretative understandings. The former is concerned only with that which is observable and hence in principle measurable. In this it is similar to Watsonian/Skinnerian psychology which abandoned the earlier attempts of psychologists to "introspect" to comprehend human behaviour. Instead, it was said, what was needed was a scientific method that considered only what was observable: and this reduced quickly to stimulus-response. An animal (usually a rat or a pigeon, but sometimes an ape or even a human being) was presented with a stimulus; the response was noted; and as a result of repeated experimentation and observation the pattern of response to stimulus could be understood.[7] The same approach is to be found in positivist approaches to behaviour in accounting/organizational situations. Only the observable is to count. As Colville (1981) has noted:

> Possible internal processes such as meanings, intentions and plans which might mediate behaviour are denied on the grounds that they cannot be observed directly. In such a formulation human behaviour becomes a function of environmental contingencies which are passively experienced. (p. 122)

That is, the contingencies can be observed and measured; the human behaviour can be observed and measured; and thus patterns can be discerned. All of this is rejected in interactionist research,[8] which emphasizes the understandings of the situations by the actors in the situations themselves: these are, by their nature,

---

[6] Yet in a way, this reading of the project of interpretation is positivist, too. By relying on unmediated observation (that is, observation that sets out to avoid a theoretical framework as a means to understanding) it places its faith in "the facts".

[7] It need hardly be said that this single sentence hardly captures the complexity of what has been the most influential school of psychology this century, though its influence now seems to be waning. Nevertheless it captures the flavour of the intention behind the school (in itself a problematic construction, since S–R psychology is suspicious of terms like "intention"!).

[8] An exception is the Iowa school of symbolic interactionism, which has specifically attempted to measure aspects of personality and relate it to social situations. This has had no impact on accounting research and we shall say no more about it here.

unobservable. We now turn to the specific proposals contained in interactionism to make this clearer.

SYMBOLIC INTERACTIONISM

There are many schools of thought that may be linked to the concerns of this chapter. Colville has listed phenomenological sociology, attribution theory, construct theory, the ethogenic approach, and dramaturgical sociology (in effect, the work of Erving Goffman), in addition to symbolic interactionism.[9] It is probably this last that has most influenced interpretive studies in accounting. We shall therefore give it the most attention, while saying a few words about some other microsociological approaches.

The Chicago school of symbolic interactionism is dependent on the insights of Cooley, Thomas, and particularly George Herbert Mead, as mediated through his student Herbert Blumer. (A positivist might conclude from this that symbolic interactionists are mostly called Herbert. This is not so.) It was Cooley who proposed the idea of the "looking glass self": that the way we perceive ourselves is the result of the way that we believe others perceive us. Thomas emphasized the importance of the "definition of the situation". "If people define a situation as real," he suggested in a famous phrase, "it is real in its consequences." However the rest of our account relies on the work of Mead and Blumer.

Blumer (1969, p.2) suggests the following central propositions of symbolic interactionism:

Human beings act towards things on the basis of the meanings that these things have for them

The "things" might be physical objects like telephones or surfboards; people individually or collectively in organizations; ideals like honesty or ambition; activities like commands or requests; and situations one encounters in everyday life.

These meanings are the result of social interaction in human society

This view has to be distinguished from two others. First, the meanings are not intrinsic properties of the things themselves. A

---

[9] Blumer tells us he invented this term in 1937 "in an offhand way" and it then "somehow caught on". He calls it a "barbaric neologism". He should know.

garden shed may have different meanings for me and for my neighbour. Second, its meaning to me is not the result of my psychological make-up; it is not the result, for instance, of my past experiences. Instead, it arises from the way I see others acting towards me with respect to the thing. It arises, that is, from my interaction with the other in perceiving its meaning.

These meanings are modified and handled through an interpretive process that is used by each individual in dealing with the signs that each encounters

The meaning of the thing does not just "come from" the interaction. It is interpreted through an active process by the person. The actor interacts with herself to indicate the things towards which she is acting; as a result, the interpretation is a matter of handling meanings. "The actor selects, checks, suspends, regroups, and transforms the meanings in the light of the situation in which he is placed and the direction of his action."

The key to action, then, is intersubjective meaning. We deal with others by attempting to understand them, and by attempting to persuade them to understand us.

Whether we are talking about groups or individuals, society comes together and consists of people interacting: that is, they act towards one another. This is the essence of society; this is why symbolic interactionists give the interaction such prominence; because everything else stems from that: "human groups or society *exists in action* and must be seen in terms of action" notes Blumer. "This picture of human society as action must be the starting point (and the point of return) for any scheme that purports to treat and analyse human society empirically" (Blumer, 1969, p. 6).

To understand this better, say the symbolic interactionists, consider two other ways we might approach an understanding of society. One is in terms of social structure. The other is in terms of culture. Yet both of these are the result of people acting towards each other; that is how they have been negotiated and expressed, and how they have come to be as they are. The trouble with other approaches, we are told, is that although they recognize the importance of interaction they then sideline it in subsequent theorizing: "they treat social interaction as merely a medium through which the determinants of behaviour pass to produce the behaviour".

When therefore we observe a particular action by someone – such as a gesture – then we read into it what we believe is the forthcoming action and plan of the actor. This means the gesture has meaning both to the person making it and the person observing it (or to whom it is made). "When the gesture has the same meaning for both, the two parties understand each other" (Blumer, p. 9).

This makes the gesture triadic in G. H. Mead's terms: it indicates the expected action by the recipient; it indicates what the actor plans to do: and "it signifies the joint action that is to arise by the articulation of the acts of both."

For example, when a consultant presents an analysis of an inventory control system to a representative of a company's management, it indicates the action expected of the recipient by the consultant (for instance, that they will read it and pass it up the managerial chain for approval); the consultant's intended action (such as to wait for board approval before taking action to implement a new inventory system and to send in a bill for work done as soon as possible); and the joint act being formed (the first stage of resolution of a consultancy assignment between them). If each party expects these things to happen, they understand each other. If the recipient throws the report in the bin, mistaking it for a superseded working paper, or if the consultant accepts a project from another company without waiting to see if they are needed to implement the new system, then the parties did not understand each other.

Thus, action only takes on a meaning when we understand the purpose behind it. The waving of my hands is in itself uninterpreted. Its meaning depends on whether I am leaning out of a train window, standing in a football crowd, or repelling an attack by a wasp. In other words, my actions normally have meanings; but those meanings can only be understood in context, and may well be understood differently by different observers (and differently again by myself). Those observers might be other people interacting with me in a social situation; they might include a researcher who later writes up her observations.

Language is the chief symbol here. We come to understand the way each of us uses words. But this is itself a social process. We interpret the language that surrounds us in a certain way because we acknowledge that it has a socially constructed meaning and that it is shared among the people around us. The term "wicked" according to the dictionary means "sinful" or "malevolent". In popular slang it can be a term of praise. The word itself therefore cannot be understood without both the context of the words surrounding it and a knowledge of who said it, and in what circumstances.

But language is in this sense twofold. We communicate with others; but we also communicate with ourselves. Each of these languages is, in a way, a dialogue. When I communicate with others, this is normally dialogical. When I communicate with myself, it is also dialogical. "I ask myself" is a common expression that reveals this in action ("I ask myself whether I can really eat this dinner").[10] What is more, when I dialogue with myself, I am both I and me. That is, I as a subjective creature dialogue with myself as me, a member of society.

Let us consider for a moment what this might mean for the organization (if we can reify the organization in this way – we shall return to this last point in a moment). The facilitative aspect should be fairly obvious: participants in an organization come to share an understanding through their mutual interaction. However, people do define their significant others (reference groups) differently within the organization; and hence different people in their different reference groups will come to consensual and stable understandings about their own position, their group's nature, and their relationship to the broader organization that differ from one group to another. To put this another way, the negotiated meaning of one group will differ from that of another group. This can cause both misunderstandings and conflict. The conflict may be the result of misunderstanding, or it might result from the clash of groups' self-defined goals.

We referred in the last paragraph to "the organization". This is clearly problematic when we are proposing a way of understanding the social world through individual social action. Put simply, once we have designated the focus of social action as being individual and group interactions, just what can we mean by an organization (or, indeed, by society)? The creation called a limited company certainly exists as a legal person, but the organization is not the same thing as the legal person: and the organization is just what is defined as the organization by the various parties who come into contact with it. We can to an extent solve the problem through suggesting that it is the participants' more or less consensual interpretations of what the organization is that governs their action towards it. This does not, on the other hand, justify our referring glibly to organizational purposes or goals as objectively or universally given.

---

[10] This is more obvious in the French. The English "I wonder" is transled as "Je me demande".

PHENOMENOLOGICAL SOCIOLOGY AND ETHNOMETHODOLOGY[11]

Phenomenological sociology draws strongly on the work of Alfred Schutz, a man who studied under the philosopher Husserl and later emigrated to the USA, to become both a part-time teacher[12] and (mainly) a banker. The hermeneutic project, by the twentieth century, had become the chief alternative to positivist natural science as a means of understanding. A key problem, as we have already seen, was the problem of perception. Husserl, like his predecessors, was concerned with the way that we make sense of the world. Now when we ask ourselves this question, the answer is inevitably rendered difficult by the fact that we have already done so. I perceive patterns in my environment (for instance, I recognize a particular shape that I see as a book), but I have already learned to do this. I have therefore already imposed particular meanings on the world: but how have I come to do so in this particular way? Husserl attempted to find an answer to this by suggesting that I should "bracket" – that is, set aside – my common-sense knowledge so as to interrogate how I came to know what I do. If successful, this would avoid the problematic conclusion that we must take truth to be what experts, through consensus based on their scientific enquiries, have concluded is true:[13] for it avoids entirely the relativism contained in the touchstone of others (cf. Bauman, 1978, p. 111). He was concerned with consciousness, which is always, and can only be, consciousness of something, "whether real or idea, whether existent or imaginary" (Gurwitsch, 1966, p. 124). To simplify the argument: if we could achieve this bracketing we could arrive through pure consciousness at a truth that did not rely either on our common sense, which

---

[11] The problem of nomenclature here is confused. I take phenomenological sociology to be constituted by the work of Schutz, and ethnomethodology to be the West Coast sociology of Cicourel, Garfinkel and others. Wells (1978, p. 275), on the other hand, refers to "ethnomethodology, or as it is now more fashionably called, phenomenological sociology". This mess need not concern us.

[12] His main work is *The Phenomenology of the Social World*; I found it interesting, but Craib engagingly calls it "one of the most boring books I have ever read".

[13] Chief among these is Karl Popper, who some accounting theorists seem to think is the last word in the philosophy of science. He relies not so much on the consensus itself as on faith that the scepticism of the scientific mind will root out errors through critical scrutiny of each new scientific proposition, and through the sounding-board of empirical testing. This is not the place for a diatribe against Popper and his naïve acolytes, however, tempting though it is.

is socialized and encumbered with our past experiences, or on the agreement of others, which is likewise potentially tainted.

Husserl's questioning went beyond cognition: but the sociology of Schutz concentrates particularly on this. As Craib (1984, p. 85) puts it:

> The basic stream of sense-experiences is meaningless – they are just there; the objects are meaningful – they have uses, names, different parts, and they signify certain things about me, that I am an academic and a writer, and certain things about other people that follow on from my being an academic or writer. Phenomenology is concerned to identify this passage from a world of meaningless sense experience to a world of meaningful objects, a passage which occurs initially in our separate individual consciousnesses and then collectively, in the interaction between consciousnesses.

Hence what chiefly distinguishes phenomenological sociology from symbolic interactionism is its insistence on delving further back into the processes of symbol formation and articulation, in which it is consciousness (whether individual or collective) that imposes order on the world, in contrast to symbolic interactionism that takes account of the individual consciousness only insofar as it enables the individual to interpret his/her social situation and social structure. This is consistent with its second difference from symbolic interactionism: for the latter is eager to get to the individual situation, and search it exhaustively for clues about "what is happening".

For Schutz, the phenomenological project seems to turn out more Lockean than Kantian:[14] for it is in the stream of consciousness that I perceive similarities among the things that I observe, and come to create typifications. These form a hierarchy, from the general (for instance, people versus inanimate objects versus moving objects) to the specific (a hod versus a shovel). But "the stocks of knowledge are not stocks of knowledge *about* the world, they are, to all practical purposes, the world itself" (Craib, p. 86). To each of us this is taken-for-granted, common-sense, knowledge that we come to share with others. This makes it the more subtle, for it is difficult to conceive of what we have learned when it is itself so "obvious".

But it is this very taken-for-grantedness that constitutes the focus of interest of ethnomethodology. This is potentially the most radical of all sociologies, because it is willing to deny so

---

[14] Which seems odd, given some of the idealist roots of Husserl's project.

much that is accepted within conventional sociology. Ethnomethodology is concerned with the nature of appearances: the way that people sustain their everyday lives (Skidmore, 1979). In this way the ethnomethodologist directs attention to the question of how a social order is possible.

Denzin (1971) puts this very well:

> Ethnomethodology takes as its basic concern analysis of the routine, taken-for-granted expectations that members of any social order regularly accept. The nature of these expectations and the form they take constitute a central focus of ethnomethodology. Basic to this perspective is the attempt to sharply distinguish scientific from everyday activity. The problems of penetrating everyday perspectives and giving them sociological explanations are repeatedly addressed, and the method of documentary analysis is set forth as a preferred strategy. The abiding concern, however, is with the relationship between everyday, taken-for-granted meanings and the organization of these meanings into routine patterns of interaction.
>
> (p. 260)

He then goes on to argue that ethnomethodology supposes that when persons interact the following assumptions are made (we shall give an example of a management accountant visiting a budgetee to negotiate the subsequent year's budget throughout):

1. It assumes that once a situation is defined, this definition holds for the duration of the encounter. Once it is clear *why* the accountant has arrived, the shared understanding is sustained throughout their discussions.
2. It is assumed that any object present in the situation is what it is presented as being. Neither person involved doubts that the document on the table is the proposed budget statement.
3. It is assumed that the meanings given an object on one occasion will hold for future occasions. If the participants view the document as crucial to the manager's future evaluation, then in any subsequent meeting that shared interpretation of the document will normally hold – or at least, be the starting point for further negotiation.
4. This leads to the point that definitions of one set of interactants are assumed to be the same as any other person or persons would develop were they in the same situation. If a different management accountant had been sent, they too would have understood the budget document in the same way.
5. Persons go through the process of identifying objects and attaching meaning to them by the use of standard terms, symbols and labels. Thus, participants are assumed to bring

with them into any situation a common vocabulary of symbols that permit the smooth flow of interaction. The management accountant does not need to explain what a variance is, and both participants know this explanation is unnecessary. It is this shared background that enables negotiation of the actual figures to take place.

6. A sixth assumption suggests that, while persons base their definitions of situations on their own biographies and past experiences, any discrepancies that might arise in an encounter because of variations in biography or experience are held in abeyance. In short, situations are defined through the process of interaction. In the case of the budget negotiation, the accountant would assume from his experience of fifteen previous meetings with other budgetees that there might be attempts to pad expenses, or to disarm him with humour, or to offer coffee at a strategic moment. This assumption would be sustained unless and until something happened to contradict it.

Ethnomethodologists, then, attempt to penetrate normal situations of interaction to uncover the rules and rituals which participants take for granted. They seek to understand how these processes proceed. In practical investigations, they often attempt to interrogate this by asking how one might disrupt normal social events so that a person's conception of the normal, real, and ordinary would be challenged.

A classic account by Garfinkel of a study he conducted through his students is worth repeating to clarify what we mean (you are encouraged to read the fascinating original (1967, pp. 47 *et seq.*)). He requested that when the students returned home they should imagine they were boarders, and act out the assumption for between fifteen minutes and an hour. "They were instructed to conduct themselves in a circumspect and polite fashion. They were to avoid getting personal, to use formal address, to speak only when spoken to." Clearly the students were going to act "nicely". Nobody could surely object to this. And yet:

> family members were stupefied. They vigorously sought to make the strange actions intelligible and to restore the situation to normal appearances. Reports were filled with accounts of astonishment, bewilderment, shock, anxiety, embarrassment, and anger, and with charges by various family members that the student was mean, inconsiderate, selfish, nasty, or impolite.

On the one hand this reaction is unsurprising; on the other hand, it is worth reflecting on how such good behaviour can be interpreted as being so unacceptable: one young woman was accused by her father of acting "like a spoiled child". The suspension of the situation, the inherent questioning through action of what is taken-for-granted, is so difficult.

In this and other experiments it was reported that the focus of interaction was soon lost when the "experimenter" attitude was assumed, and for all practical purposes the students were unable to carry on normal interaction. Garfinkel explained this inability with the concept of trust. This he defined as the assumption on the part of any person that all others he encounters will share his expectations and definition of the situation.

A further strain of ethnomethodology has been to show how phenomena are created through definition. An example was Cicourel's work on juvenile delinquency. He showed how a delinquent has to be defined – that what makes a person a delinquent rather than a non-delinquent has to be negotiated. This is the result of conversations with the youth (before they are defined as delinquent), with parents, arresting policeman, a counsellor, and judge. These conversations are translated into official reports: these define whether the youth is or is not a delinquent. Cases may be ambiguous; then patterns are defined from the experience of those involved to help in the categorization. In other words, we do not have set categories of "delinquent" and "non-delinquent" as such: delinquency is pieced together.

We may argue that a management control system exists, in part, to create precisely these kinds of definition. Budgetees have to be sifted and understood as those who keep to their budgets and manage well, through to those who are "delinquent" – that is, poor managers. What defines a poor manager will be a confluence of hearsay on interpersonal skills, on economic performance in absolute terms, on keeping to budget, on conforming to social expectations (dress, recreations), and so on. The accounting system, therefore, is part of the ongoing definition of what a poor manager is; and it is part of the taken-for-granted in itself (that is, people take it for granted that they know what an adverse variance is, and when it shades from acceptable through borderline to unacceptable). There is to the ethnomethodologist no unproblematic categorization of a good or bad manager. Bad managers are negotiated, not pre-existing.

WHERE HAVE WE GOT SO FAR? ALL OF THIS, AND ACCOUNTING TOO

It is time to take stock. It should be clear that we have not, in any of the above, been proposing a theory, or indeed, a set of theories. The assumptions tend to be metaphysical; they are appeals to our need to understand, which then provide suggested frameworks within which we can understand the action of the social situation. They are insights from sociology, which has bothered to reflect at length about the philosophical foundations of its knowledge base (more so than either, say, economics or political science). We may now address the question of their relevance to, and use within, the academic literature of management accounting.

Unlike financial accounting, management accounting is intended to affect the internal processes of the organization. It seeks not only to change people's behaviour (through standard costs and budgets – what text writers like to call accounting for control) – but also to change their *consciousness*; it seeks to make them "cost-conscious", and more amenable to control, because that is necessary for the benefit of the employer. Now management does of course relate to its accounting systems, just as managers relate to each other. Financial control systems affect managerial behaviour, since they affect both managerial interactions in the context of accounting information and also managerial behaviour overtly faced with accounting information. Accounting thus becomes one aspect of the definition of the situation referred to by the symbolic interactionists. It also becomes, it must be said, part of the taken-for-granted context of normal organizational life.

We are also now confronted with a key question about the action approach to understanding organizational situations involving management accounting: why might this research not prove useful in the same way as traditional and systems approaches? Why, at the beginning of this chapter, did we suggest that its motivation and possibilities are quite different? Of course, there is no logical reason to claim that, just because people have not customarily investigated the accounting situation with an intention to improve systems performance, therefore their research cannot be used in this way. This does bring us to a problem at the heart of the action framework in the context of accounting: can we use the *verstehende* insights of interactive studies to improve our prescriptions for future design, that is, extrapolate from one study to a series of future similar situations, or are such situations unique in such a way that they do not permit their own use for prescriptions? There is no simple answer to this; and indeed, there are lively differences of opinion. We may briefly explain how each side of the argument might run.

VIEW I: In favour of prescription and extrapolation

We may argue this view as follows. Any situation will have aspects that are unique to it, and aspects that are general. For an example of the latter, if the subject is a budget negotiation, then there will tend to be factors such as self-protection by the budgetee, second-guessing for bias by the superior, and so on. The former (unique) factors may act as noise, and be acknowledged to create a (more or less conventional) error term; but the latter can be observed and used to predict how other managers faced with similar situations might act and react. The method itself permits more depth of understanding than conventional empiricist methods; but far from acting as a barrier to extrapolation, this just improves the quality of the research and thus permits the extrapolation to be better than it would be with conventional methods. At heart, the nature of interpretive studies is one in which a better means of understanding the situation is employed, but once this has been achieved, the normal rules of science apply, which are that given the objectivity within the situation itself (however complex, it is in the last analysis just an event to be understood) it must be possible to learn from it for future such situations.

VIEW II: Against prescription and extrapolation

We may argue the counter-view as follows. The very nature of each social encounter is highly complex. It is unique, in that the particular people involved in the particular situation will interpret it in a particular way. That reflexive, unique understanding will lead not only to a definition of the situation unique to its actors, but will ensure that no other situation can be quite the same, if only because each such social encounter is defined in its own terms. A useful analogy with the empiricist method of factor analysis may clarify this. The factors generated and the factor loadings in any given empirical study are by their nature a function of the particular event; and hence a replication of the event can never lead to a replication of the factors precisely because they were generated by the unique circumstances of that particular set of observations. However, with interactionist accounts the problem is more severe, just because quantification is mostly alien to their intent. A social situation *unfolds*. At each point in that unfolding a new, and not necessarily determined, interpretation of the situation arises. To encapsulate what happened as a guide to what might happen in a similar circumstance is to do violence to the social construction that took place. It imports an alien notion (replicability) into a means of understanding that has no place for it. This can be seen by going back to the earliest hermeneutic roots of the action framework, in which "immersion in the spirit of the age" was deemed so important. We now have immersion in the spirit of the managerial encounter: and that in itself is quite contrary to the objectified attempted replication of a situation.

We cannot resolve this question here (though my inclination is to support View II). It is clearly important, if only because an acceptance of View I will enable interpretive research to be brought within the fold of managerial studies – in the sense that managerial studies are studies to improve management. View II returns the studies to the realm of social science, concerned with understanding *to understand understanding*. We learn how people construct their realities. We do not thereby tell them how to act next time.

SOME ACCOUNTING STUDIES

When we turn briefly to particular studies in the accounting literature that are best described as being interpretive, we must make a matter clear at the outset. Although most of the researchers are well aware of the background described above, they did not necessarily subscribe to any or all these ideas; nor were they necessarily content not to go beyond them. Thus, although the reader may understand our introduction to these interpretive approaches, s/he should expect that this understanding may possibly prove inadequate – research studies normally attempt to push their theoretical framework beyond something that is already in the literature and thus is "not new knowledge"; and be prepared for some ideas perhaps running contrary to what we have said up to now.

The series of accounting studies that most closely follow symbolic interactionism and similar interpretive frameworks are those carried out at the University of Bath (cf. Colville, 1981 and Tomkins and Groves, 1983, for theoretical discussions; and Rosenberg, Tomkins and Day, 1982 and Rosenberg, 1989 for empirical studies).

The Rosenberg, Tomkins and Day study concerns the movement of finance professionals within a local authority, and it links to the sociology of the professions. The methods used were a combination of participants' own stories and observation by the researchers themselves (one of the named authors was himself a full-time employee of a local authority). The paper reconstructs the self-image of the accounting staff concerned, their negotiated image of their role in the local authority, and their constructions of the nature of the local authority itself. The paper considers also the impact on the departments of the staff moving; and this too reflects a theoretical acknowledgement that this impact is the result of an unfolding of reciprocal expectations by the organization and by the employee. In these ways the paper reflects the theoretical framework presented here. It is concerned less with the impact of accounting information itself on people directly – with the way that accounting is

> intimately involved in the creation of meanings . . . [and] provides a particular set of categories through which individuals and organizations can order and structure their world.
>
> (Dent, 1986, pp. 150–1)

That is more evident in Rosenberg (1989), whose paper considers the way that accounting reconstructs the way the county treasurer and other budget officials view and undertake their task, and additionally the way the politics of budget setting reconstructs the annual budget itself. The paper can be interpreted as suggesting that there is no "real" budget out there to be created by the budget officers based on the need to allocate appropriate resources, keep within government constraints, or whatever. Rather, there is a negotiated reality which unfolds over the budget-setting period. Some political actions are "objective" in the sense that if X forbids Y to spend on an activity and has a right to do so under the legitimate rules of the system, then that is a concrete fact. But this is rare; for in any case, all parties would realize the possibilities for virement or creative accounting of some kind to circumvent the rules. More common is a negotiation *in the light of acknowledged differential locations of power.* These are of course the results of the reciprocal interpretations we have discussed already.

A somewhat different study is that of Roberts (1989). This considers a series of episodes in the career of Clare, who worked in telephone sales, and her reactions to managerial manipulation. Clare's attitude to her job at different periods of these episodes is interrogated, and contextualized into the culture of a hard-driving telephone sales organization. By concentrating on one person, Roberts reduces the scope of his understanding of the organizational context: but through the resulting depth he teases out subtleties in the way reciprocal expectations can be overturned through organizational dynamics and the contrasts between personal goals and corporate targets. The setting of quantitative targets develops in managers a competitiveness that leads to discontinuities between what they expect and what others expect them to expect. Thus the system of explicit goals interacts with managerial ambition and personal relationships; the results are capable of being personally damaging.

Nahapiet's study (1988) considers resource allocation within an area of the UK's National Health Service, discussing "how the new accounting both shaped and was in turn shaped by organizational reality . . . [so that] the relationship between accounting and organizational processes is reflexive, with each defining and being defined by the other." What is especially interesting here, as in the Rosenberg study, is the way that researchers both feel the need to combine the insights of interpretive theorizing with understanding the organization and its operations as a whole, and perceive no difficulty in doing so. I write this because commentators on interpretive studies criticize them for providing no means to move from the particular understanding of the situation to the broader social context. What is the bridge, it is asked, that enables us to use the insights gained for an analysis of broader society? One answer is that the latter common-sense phenomenon cannot be taken as a "thing" in itself to be understood, that perhaps the action analysis is itself something beyond which we cannot expect to go, and that the "obvious" structures of society are actually no such thing. These studies in management control, however, appear to find no difficulty in using interpretation to interrogate an organizational and financial control system. Nahapiet not only references Berger and Luckmann's classic book on interactive sociology, but also claims that her study, being concerned

> with the use of language and other symbols for expressive purposes . . . concludes with a consideration of accounting as a language for discourse, a set of rules for negotiating an understanding of organizational reality and a mechanism for establishing and maintaining the legitimacy of social action.

CONCLUSION

Perhaps we have not emphazised sufficiently the extent to which interpretive frameworks have shown how management accounting studies can move beyond the elementary notion that management accounting is primarily a set of techniques. Once we have left the traditional world of accounting, and once we have similarly abandoned the attempt to design accounting systems so as to optimize the operations of organizational systems, we find we can both interrogate the processes through which people negotiate their reality, and also the way that negotiation is filtered through the mechanisms of the demands of the accounting systems of which they must take cognizance. Interactionist studies are at heart particularistic. In the language of critique they are designated reductionist, in the sense that they build pictures of society from individual interactions between and among people. Thus, the criticism goes, they imply that society is just the sum of the interactive negotiations as understood and consensualized by individuals.

Drawing on passages in the previous section there are perhaps two possible responses to this. One is to suggest that, ultimately, perhaps this is all there is; and there are no grounds to suppose otherwise, save common sense, which is hardly a category to aid understanding of something so complex as society and its institutions. The other response is to suggest that, once we have made sense of the interpretive acts that infuse accounting in use within organizations, then we have a springboard from which to better reconstruct a coherence from the complexity of organizational phenomena with which we are confronted. This is not quite the same thing as adhering to the "replicability" to which we gave attention earlier. It is, however, a hopeful note insofar as any reader may show impatience with anything so apparently modest as the attempt to understand "the interaction" in the context of "the accounting information".

DISCUSSION QUESTIONS

1. What kinds of insight into the operation of accounting control systems can we gain from action approaches that are not available from traditional/systems views?
2. What questions might we wish to ask about accounting systems that interactionist approaches cannot answer?

3. Do you believe you can use interactionist insights to develop better control systems (be careful to ensure you are clear that what you mean by "better" is reconcilable with interactionism)?

4. Describe how accounting information contributes to structuring an interaction. What elements of the information do you think are taken-for-granted?

5. Suppose a board of directors decides to abandon a company's standard cost system. The chief accountant objects. What insights have you gained from this chapter that might help you to explain the accountant's objections?

6. Go through the six assumptions of ethnomethodology, applying them to a set of group discussion questions on a chapter about action approaches to management accounting (that is, perhaps what you are doing right now).

7. Some years ago I was at a conference when one of the first interactionist studies on accounting was presented. A representative of one of the major accountancy bodies criticized the study on the grounds that it was "too theoretical", and should have had more detail on cost methods, etc. (that is, it was a criticism from the traditional school). The researchers responded that they had presented the paper to the senior financial managers of the industry concerned, and had been told it was the first academic study that had really communicated itself to them as representing "what really went on". Do you think this response was adequate?

8. Do you think interactionist approaches view people as rational?

4

Stories From Below: The Radical Critique

When we considered the systems approach in Chapter 2, we observed that we can consider systems in society as nested. The department or division at the highest resolution level is within the corporate system, the corporate system is within the nation's social system, and this in turn is within the international political and social system. Since these systems are nested, we would expect phenomena that apply in society beyond the organization to be true within the organization too. For example, it is trite to observe that the accounting system of an enterprise within a socialist planned economy would be different from the accounting system in a privately-owned company operating in a market economy. This may be generalized: features of the social and political system affect our understanding of the individual organization and its accounting system.

This means that the way we make sense of our society must affect the way we analyse the operation of the organization and the accounting system within it. Traditional management accounting theory is anchored in a framework that views society as pluralist, that is, one in which there are various competing interest groups that come into conflict as they struggle for power. According to the simplest form of pluralist theory (for a discussion of some variants of pluralist political theory, see Tinker, 1984), the political and social system is a fair game: sometimes some groups get what they want, sometimes others. For example, a pluralist might point to changes of government (Labour versus Conservative; Democrat versus Republican) as evidence of changes in the locus of power and influence. Similarly, the influence of the green movement increased in Europe over the 1980s, at the same time as the visible influence of the trade unions (in the UK, at any rate) declined. This view is consistent with a homeostatic systems view of society, which adjusts (but still, essentially, in steady state) to new circumstances. It can also quickly shade into functionalism, by supposing that, since society has taken this turn, it therefore follows that it *should have done* so as to sustain equilibrium in the face of a changed internal and/or external environment.

As we pointed out in Chapter 1, the fact that political pluralism is taken for granted means that it is never stated explicitly in conventional management accounting thought. However, it is reflected in the implicit belief about the nature of the business enterprise. Conventional theorizing understands the organization as essentially a co-operative venture in which the various interest groups come together to achieve some purpose (remember, systems theory views organizations as teleological). This implies that there can be common goals among the interest groups (for example, that a competitive market price which carves out a high market share is advantageous to employers, employees and suppliers of raw material alike). The corollary is that the management accounting system can be so designed as to be of mutual benefit to all the parties involved in the firm. If the accountant discovers inefficiencies through standard cost variance analysis, then it is helpful to all parties, because the avoidance of these inefficiencies improves the firm's competitive position and thereby secures the interests of all who depend upon it.

To make the link clearer, consider the opposite situation. If the true nature of the political system beyond the work organization were one of a permanent hierarchy, in which one class systematically ruled over and exploited another class from generation to generation, then these power and economic asymmetries would be reflected in the organization. This too would consist of permanent exploitation of some by others; and then we would understand the nature of the management accounting system quite differently. We would not expect a natural consensus, in which we could explain to those policed by their budget systems that this was for their own benefit because it kept their company afloat and prosperous and thus contributed to their own welfare. Instead, we should have to view the budget and costing systems as sophisticated control mechanisms that were designed to ensure the institutionalized subordination of labour to the needs of capital.

It is because of this link between the nature of the socio-economic system and the nature and function of the management accounting system in the organization that we have to pay attention especially in this chapter to a theorizing of society as a whole, and cannot fall back on a reductionist focus on the organization and its participants alone. When we turn to the schools of thought to be covered in this chapter, the assumption of pluralism is challenged. Market societies, far from being pluralist, are seen to be structured in such a way that certain elites or classes (these are not the same thing) have power, use that power for their own ends, and retain that power across generations (this last is often referred to as the "reproduction" of such structural inequalities, since what is true at one period of time is reproduced at the next period through the medium of the structure concerned). Structural inequality, both in terms of the economy and in terms of power, is endemic. Indeed it is more than endemic; it is an intrinsic and inherent feature of modern Western societies.[1]

To make this clear, we distinguish two competing models of modern Western society:

An industrial society

This view is theorized by taking the mode of production to be the chief distinguishing feature, and sees societies such as our own as being different from, say, feudal societies, because of the differences in the level of technology. Since technology is the driving force, such an approach can bypass problems of social relations and concentrate instead on how to optimize the use of that technology. That is in effect what traditional management accounting does: it asks no questions about ends, but focuses on the technology of the means. Activity-based costing provides a good example here.

A capitalist society

The alternative model views modern society as one in which the relations of production among owners of capital, land and wage-labour are at least equally significant. The defining characteristic

---

[1] There is a useful technical term to describe this, "immanent".

is then the employment relation, and what this relation means for each party involved – landowner, owner of capital, and provider of labour power. The traditional techniques of management accounting have nothing to say on this subject.

So long as our society is characterized mainly by its technology (the former theory), there are, in principle, opportunities to level out inequalities of opportunity. True pluralism can be achieved by refining the way institutions operate. Any damaging conflict is believed not to be immanent to the system, but to be a problem that can be ironed out. In contrast, once it is acknowledged that our society is structured by relations that inherently follow from the employment relation (the second approach), inequality becomes inescapable. To put this another way, once we have moved from the view of the organization as one of co-operation and common ends, to one in which the owners of the enterprise exploit those working in it by appropriating the surplus gained from their labour, then we are obliged to conclude that the nature of the organization is different, reflecting a society that is different, and hence that the function of management accounting is different.

In this chapter we consider approaches to accounting in organizations that begin with the proposition that structural inequality characterizes society. This means we have to theorize the role of management accounting in the organization very differently in this chapter from the characterization proposed in Chapters 2 and 3.

I shall treat the radical approach to management accounting on the basis that it has tended to develop in two ways. One of these starts from, and concentrates on, the material conditions of the labour process within the industrial organization, and the way that this constitutes a microcosm of the economic function in society. The other is more concerned with the way this economic condition is intertwined with the linguistic and symbolic super-structure, and the way that this comes to constitute the reproduction of society. I propose to begin, however, with some general comments on the way the radical critique of society has been formulated as an alternative to conventional accounts of the nature of liberal democracy.

I must also briefly explain why I shall go about this exposition through a critique of other theoretical positions, rather than just presenting it as it is. This approach is a feature of the radical position. Traditional theory is based on building blocks: on the idea that we can start with evidence about the nature of the world, theorize the regularities that we observe, and from there move to other regularities, building upon our existing knowledge.[2] The critical approach is sceptical about the transparency of observation, since there are, as we shall see, no value-neutral social facts. Hence it develops knowledge of the world through engaging in a continual dialogue with what appears to be the case. Indeed we could, to simplify initially, typify the difference in the development of knowledge between the two as being the difference between the monological (here is a truth that I shall tell you based on the hard facts) and the dialogical (let us subject truth claims to critique and seek knowledge through investigating the inconsistencies that result).

Finally, as with the other schools of thought treated in this book, we must say something briefly about the genesis of the ideas underlying the various radical positions. Inevitably, this must begin with a consideration of the place of Marx as an influence on radical thinking, and thus as an influence on radical accounting. There had of course been writers and political movements before Marx that had subjected the inequalities of their societies to criticism and proposed social change. You will be aware of the Peasants' Revolt, the Levellers and the Chartists from the most cursory study of British history. These political movements from below tended to lack any coherent political strategy, and they certainly lacked any coherent theory. The earliest major body of socialist thinking came from France: and in particular, the likes of Saint-Simon, Fourier and Proudhon. These were relatively systematic, being explicated in often quite extensive written works. However their chief defect (particularly in the case of Fourier) was their Utopian character: they identified problems in the society around them, and designed societies they believed would be better. Marx's work was distinguished from

---

[2] At this point, those aware of Popper's philosophy of science may object that, given the widespread acceptance of Popper's ideas among practising researchers, this is not the common picture of how knowledge develops. According to Popper, theory must precede observation, since otherwise there is no means of knowing what to observe. However, Popper's idea of theory and observation differs from the position here in a number of significant respects; and it has in common with inductive observational theory its contention that value-neutral observation and measurement is possible through the operations of the community of scientists. It is still therefore a building-block approach: and it is this that will be challenged in the radical critique.

them by its proposed scientific nature.[3] Far from merely proposing a better system, Marx was concerned to explicate the laws of history and to do so in the light of his knowledge of (as has often been remarked) German philosophy, French socialism and British political economy. Marx did not describe in detail his conception of how an ideal society should be. However, he did synthesize in a unique way a theory of philosophy, history, economics, politics and sociology in developing his ideas; and since his death his system has influenced writers not only in all these disciplines but also in anthropology, archaeology, divinity, human geography, law, linguistics – and accounting.

Marxist theory has developed quite markedly since Marx's death; however, to begin to label radical work as Marxist, neo-Marxist, or post-Marxist is, in the end, a pointless task leading only to ultimately self-defeating discussions along the lines of "what Marx really meant" or, even worse, "what Marx might have said had he lived to see . . .". The radical project has developed in so many revealing and overlapping ways that we need only say that a dialogue with Marx is inevitable – his influence has been so far-reaching.[4] Thus the account we shall now give is neither Marxist nor non-Marxist: it is rather a set of complementary ideas, frequently informed by the work of Marx and his successors, that are common to the approach taken by radical accounting writers.

FUNDAMENTALS OF THE RADICAL CRITIQUE

The production of goods and services is social production. It is the result of the confluence of efforts of various kinds by productive members of society: for, because of specialization both within the individual enterprise and among enterprises, no

---

[3] It was Proudhon who popularized the expression "property is theft", though he was not the first to use it. Marx was scornful of such ideas, seeing them as infantile and ungrounded in a proper scientific understanding of history. However, we get into deep water here since there is an extensive Marxist debate on the extent to which Marx's project was undermined by the immanent contradictions caused by his insistence on a certain conception of science (disparagingly known as *scientism*). This debate is beyond our scope.

[4] It is interesting to observe that in the social sciences (with only economics, accounting and psychology as exceptions) a study of Marxist concepts has been an essential part of any scholar's education. The resilience in institutionalizing ignorance of these ideas in economics and accounting in particular makes an interesting subject for the sociology of knowledge.

individual can produce alone to any significant extent. In contrast, the rewards that are paid out to producers are individual rewards. Employees receive wages and salaries individually, for example: whatever employee X receives is not available to any other employee. These two factors are thus potentially in conflict: because, given that no individual can produce without the co-operation of others, and each individual expects some recompense as an individual contributor, some means of allocating the fruits of social production is necessary.

In capitalist society this is achieved by the market. Consider the following passage (which is not a direct quotation, but conflated to reflect the standard propositions of neoclassical marginalist economics):

Markets are the mechanisms that are used in our economy to resolve the above problem of allocating resources; and they do this through prices. Neoclassical economic theory explains how prices are arrived at through the decisions of independent buyers and sellers. This is necessary because of scarcity: and the price mechanism is the appropriate way of allocating goods and services, because it ensures that those who want them most and are prepared to back this up with payment, receive them. At the same time the mechanism favours the efficient producers who can keep their costs down: because through the profits that are reported to the financial markets they will be rewarded with fresh funds to invest. Thus the efficient prosper and the inefficient do not.

Now there is not a statement in this paragraph that cannot be subjected to a searching radical critique: and that is where we shall begin.

For a start, this passage seems to assume that markets are, if not perfect, then at least not too far from being perfect markets. Yet many industries are monopolistic or oligopolistic; they operate cartels when they can; and there is abundant evidence of the efforts of industry to keep it that way through barriers to entry (for evidence, see any textbook on industrial economics). An oligopolistic supplier is in a strong position to set prices, so that profits do not reflect efficiency. This in turn means that if capital does indeed flow where there are high profits, it is not necessarily flowing towards the most efficient producers.

Consumers are not individuals who are unambiguously free to choose, either. In the first place, massive amounts are spent on advertising and promotion by producers to ensure that individuals do not follow their "natural tastes". Indeed, we may challenge the whole idea of "natural tastes", if by this we mean wants that are separate from the socialization that results from manipulating the consumer. If producers make what consumers want as revealed by their expenditure patterns, why continually market new products, the need for which is not apparent from the human condition (such as yet another kind of chocolate bar, or seventeen variants on one basic model of car)? An individual consumer is supposed by neoclassical economic theory to be autonomous, selecting on the basis of personal preferences. These preferences are argued to arise from their tastes as independent individuals, as expressed through their individual utility functions. But those individuals have grown up in society; their tastes and beliefs have been heavily influenced by society: and hence they are not independent at all, but rather are the socialized results of the network of marketing structures employed by corporate profit-making enterprises. Indeed, this brings us to the second objection to the notion of the free individual with natural tastes: people are inherently social beings. Back in Chapter 1 we pointed out the problems associated with theorizing economics through Robinson Crusoe. This can be greatly extended. No one grows up except through society. Thus what we are as we develop is to a major extent what we are moulded into by society (socialization). To suggest that after a lifetime of socialization any person is a wholly autonomous individual with an independent preference ordering is at the very least highly questionable.

Once the sovereign consumer has disappeared, the rationale for the supremacy of the market as servant of the consumer must also disappear. It is less seductive when we replace the idea of the sovereign consumer with the sovereign nexus of wants derived from producers' marketing and general socialization: to say, "We satisfy the wants we created" is far less persuasive than saying, "We satisfy the wants of our customers". A critique has, then, led us to begin to question the most basic tenet of the justification for accepting the demands of the market mechanism.

Once the idea of the market as the neutral arbitrator of the allocation of resources has dissolved, we have to question afresh the nature of the production function. Indeed, this brings us to the heart of the difference between the traditional neoclassical economic model and the radical model which has many of its roots in the classical economics of Smith and Ricardo. The neoclassical model begins with markets; and we might almost say it ends with markets. There are not just product markets but also factor markets (for labour, in particular); and general equilibrium theory is concerned with bringing all these together. In parallel, much of the traditional economic model concerned with operations within the firm takes the firm to operate wholly within the constraints of the external markets, and generates notions of quasi-markets within the firm (see Hirschleifer's analysis in the transfer pricing literature, for instance).

The radical, Marxist model does not begin with markets at all, but with production. With its roots in the history of social relations, it prefers to focus on the employment relation. Markets are viewed as epiphenomenal. There was individual production before there were either employment relationships or product markets: the earliest peoples produced to survive. Let Mandel (1969) then take up the story (sadly his sexist language was endemic even among radicals twenty years ago):

> As long as the productivity of labor remains at a level where one man can only produce enough for his own subsistence, *social* division does not take place and any social differentiation within society is impossible. Under these conditions, all men are producers and they are all on the same economic level.
>
> Every increase in the productivity of labor beyond this low point makes a small surplus possible, and once there is a surplus of products . . . then the conditions have been set for a struggle over how this surplus will be shared.
>
> From this point on, the total output of a social group no longer consists solely of labor necessary for the subsistence of the producers. Some of this labor output may now be used to release a section of society from having to work for its own subsistence.
>
> Whenever this situation arises, a section of society can become a ruling class, whose outstanding characteristic is its emancipation from the need of working for its own subsistence.

This then created the conditions for the struggle over the surplus from labour. Marxist economic models are based around ideas of *value*. Neoclassical models are interested in price, and tend to relegate questions of value to questions of price – the normal formulation is that something is only worth what someone will pay for it. But once attention is switched to value, then the way value is created and the way the output of the creation/production process is distributed become problematic. To illustrate this we consider the question of wage payments.

Anchored in markets, neoclassical models explain the level of wages paid in any given organization by reference to the labour market, and appeal to notions such as the marginal productivity of labour within the context of this market. In a shallow sense, we could object that labour markets are not free and open, that marginal productivity in the case of, say, a marketing director's salary is remarkably difficult to assess, and that labour markets are plagued by various kinds of inefficiencies. But that is a minor problem, because it is still rooted in the notion of the market as the starting point. Instead, radical theory asks about the process of production and thus the creation of value. The employee produces value; (s)he is paid some fraction of that value in wages: and the rest accrues to the firm's owners. Since it is in the owners' interest to maximize the value extracted from the employee, the function of the management accounting system, control of which is in the hands of the owners' agents, the management, is clearly not for the mutual benefit of all the parties involved, but rather for the benefit of the owners (this view of the employment relationship was not newly developed by Marx, but was stated very clearly by Adam Smith some decades earlier).

The idea of the surplus value created by the employee being expropriated by the owners thus dissolves the idea of any possible fairness in wage and price levels: it also leads inevitably to the employee's being exploited by the owner (capitalist). As to fairness, we are left with no basis for language such as "a fair day's work for a fair day's pay", because there can be no concept of fairness where there are no neutral and fair market mechanisms. As to exploitation, the perceptive reader may suppose there is an objection to this stage of the argument: namely, that the surplus value is going to the shareholders and other providers of capital as a reward for their "waiting", and through the opportunity cost of the use of their funds. Although we cannot go into the full complexities of the rebuttal of this here, we may note two arguments. First, that if there is no "fair day's work for a fair day's pay" for the employee because of the nature of the employee relation, social power relations, and the imperfection of markets, then it follows that there can similarly be no notion of the proper return to capital (for the controversies over capital theory see Tinker (1980)). Second, labour is essential for the reproduction – that is, the continuation – of the economy in society. Labour is needed both to sustain current existence and to provide the means for future production, through producing value that can be crystallized into capital for the future. Capital is needed, in other words; capitalists are not. Their existence results from the relations of production, and not from any technical need.

THE STATE

We have looked at the way radical theory arrives at the conclusion that one class of people exploits another class through the employment relationship. We have had to simplify outrageously, and limitations of space have prevented us from considering explanations of other classes in society (although we shall later meet a radical analysis of the role of the corporate manager). Nevertheless we have glimpsed the way this class relation in society is reflected in the work organization, and vice versa. We now move beyond this *economic* relation to broader political relations: and this means we must now turn to the role of the State.

In a modern society characterized by economic markets, the State is clearly a major institution. Employers do not, as such, have many votes (capital in its abstract form has no votes at all). Employees, on the other hand, have the great bulk of the power of voting for a government to represent them. It might be supposed therefore that the State, which is controlled by the elected government, would operate in favour of the workforce and against the forces of capital that are exploiting them. This supposition, however, would be mistaken.

There are a number of reasons according to radical theory why this is so. Suppose we defined the State as the most obvious set of institutions: government ministries, local government, and the facilities they control, such as the army and the police. These are semi-autonomous institutions. They are staffed with people who have their own beliefs, needs and interests. More perhaps: for just as the systems theory of Chapter 2 acknowledges that organizations (that is, organizational systems) can have goals separate from the goals of the people within them, so radical theory proposes that the State has interests in its own survival and prosperity.[5] The State then takes actions that sustain the existing economic system, since it is the system that has led to the development of the modern State, and it is part of the economic surplus from that economic system that is used to pay for the State. Thus the State does not act in the interests of capital

---

[5] I am severely simplifying here. There has been an extensive literature on the role of the State, within which many have argued that the State can only be an arm of powerful interests: that, in other words, since capital is in control, it follows that the State necessarily acts in the interest of capital. The approach in the text is now the more commonly accepted one. See, for example, Holloway and Picciotto, 1978 and Jessop, 1982.

as such: it acts to sustain the capitalist system which (indirectly) benefits the interests of capital.

All this can be possible both because the government of the day has relatively little impact on the total set of functions of the State, and because the ramifications of the State extend beyond the boundaries of those functions overtly funded through the public purse.

As to the first, we could begin with the popular image of Sir Humphrey Appleby in the popular television programme *Yes, Minister*, a civil servant who (mostly successfully) attempts to control "his" minister. Helpful though this is in the particular, it is nevertheless a reductionist depiction. It is better to seek to understand the continuity of power of the State irrespective of the political party in power not only through the way in which the State manages information and hence affects policy, but also through the State's interest in stability. Any attempt by a government to act is generally an attempt to change, and the effects of change are difficult to predict. When, therefore, state officials are content with the fruits of a social configuration, there will be no obvious pay-off to social change.

This may seem an unnecessarily complex explanation; but any simpler formulation runs up against the paradox that the powerful leaders of the state apparatus, permanent state officials at the top of the hierarchy, are generally reckoned to be mainly conservative in political outlook; and yet it was the conservative administrations of Thatcher and Reagan that publicly proposed the cutting down of state power, whereas their opponents, in the name of social justice, were generally believed to be in favour of extending the role of the State.

Turning to the second point, the picture of the State as being just that part of society directly linked to government is a distortion because it confuses the concrete "who is responsible to whom" in the formal textbooks of government with the underlying reality of social forces. Just as we had to distinguish capital from labour earlier as underlying forces (otherwise we would have no way of resolving the problem of the employee who has shares in the company), so we have to distinguish the totality of the State from those funded by taxation and administered by those we elect. To do otherwise would cause intractable problems. For example, suppose that the practices of external accounting were regulated by a ministry of trade (as happens in many countries). Then accounting regulation would be rightly defined as a state function. Suppose instead it were regulated by a formally independent body such as the Accounting Standards Board (UK) or the Financial Accounting Standards Board (USA). Is it, or is it not, a state function in those countries? After all, the people involved as regulators would be from the same social classes, would be drawn from pools of similar expertise and would act with much the same intentions. Yet if we restricted our definition of the State to the civil service we would exclude the latter while including the former. It is better therefore to define the State in terms of *what it does*. Among other things the State regulates civil society. Thus whatever its funding or its personnel, we would include the accounting regulators as part of the State.[6]

Now before we move on to the next stage of the overall radical framework, it is worth while considering why a discussion of the State might be important to students of management accounting. One answer would be that the State implicates itself in social control, right down to calculative practices for individual companies' internal accounting systems in a country such as France, under the *Plan Comptable*. This may be dismissed as an exception. However, the State has also been implicated in the development of cost accounting within its own munitions factories during the First World War (Loft, 1986); private enterprise contracting for the government finds its costing methods important, given the possibility of cost-plus contracting, especially in the case of the defence industries: companies facing price controls have to justify price increases by reference to levels of profits, which change depending on cost accounting methods for, say, inventory measurement: but most importantly, we return to our systemic argument that the institutions and relations of society imbue those within the individual organization. We shall see later that we may explain the actions of those who obtain control of the organization and operate its accounting systems through understanding the relationship between the State and professional associations.

As the final plank in the construction of the radical framework, we return to extend a matter we discussed earlier, namely, the importance of socialization. When we describe the citizen as "socialized" we mean that they have come to learn both through the unconscious assimilation of the social world around them and through the conscious inculcation of concepts from family and schooling. They learn what is appropriate behaviour in given circumstances in the microsocial realm; and they also take in ideas

---

[6] The reader may earlier have noticed, perhaps with a tinge of exasperation, that I have nowhere defined "the State". The reason should by now I hope be clear: what it is depends on how it is conceptualized. I have observed the same reluctance to define the State in the sources from political science that I have used.

about the nature of the broader society of which they are a part – for example, its religious beliefs, political system and cultural web. It is a common-place in sociology to suggest that the individual is created by society rather more than society is created by the individual. However, we now move beyond this position to enquire into the source of the ideas through which we as social persons come to believe what we do.

Ideas do not exist in a vacuum. They are created and disseminated by people and groups. However, they clearly cannot be attributed to those people and groups in any individualistic way since, first, those people were themselves socialized before they produced their ideas and second, they will be acceptable neither to publisher nor to reader (if written, of course) unless they strike some chord in at least one segment of society – and each of these is equally a result of socialization. Thus although we may attribute ideas to individuals for convenience (also to massage their egos and, in the case of academic writers, to enhance their promotion prospects) their significance is as social ideas.[7] Now a capitalist system is a system of power in which the providers and controllers of capital are inevitably in the ascendant. Since this system is reproduced across generations without any significant challenge, there must be an explanation for the apparent willingness of the subjects of the power relationship to accede to it and to make no attempt to change it either through their political voting or through direct action.

The explanation lies in the key significance of ideas in moulding the way people view their world. Those ideas as a whole will be ideas that are supportive of the system, and generally ideas that mask the underlying exploitative relationship. They will be, in a word, ideologies. Marx's description of this can hardly be bettered:

> The ideas of the ruling class are, in every age, the ruling ideas: i.e. the class which is the dominant *material* force in society is at the same time its dominant *intellectual* force. The class which has the means of material production at its disposal, has control at the same time over the means of mental production, so that in consequence the ideas of those who lack the means of mental production are, in general, subject to it.
>
> (Marx, 1978, p. 172)

---

[7] Marx (1978) put it succinctly: "Life is not determined by consciousness, but consciousness by life."

This is of course a different use of the term "ideology" from that in everyday society, which tends to treat ideologies as something marginal, to be avoided by proper-thinking people. Shils, in the *International Encyclopedia of the Social Sciences* remarks that "ideologies . . . are not usually espoused by the incumbents and custodians of the central institutional and value systems", and that "All ideologies – whether progressive or traditionalistic, revolutionary or reactionary – entail an aggressive alienation from the existing society." A radical would expect an "authoritative" voice to say that. An apologist for the current system would be expected to marginalize radical ideas by defining language (the use of the term) in this way. Hence this statement is itself an ideological act.[8]

In its simplest form, then, we draw from this discussion of ideology the claim that the real material conditions in which people live can be hidden from them by the matrix of ideas with which they are surrounded. If the media (television, press and accounting textbooks included) are all imbued with the tacit understanding that our society is pluralist and basically fair, and more, that this society and its social order are part of the natural order of things, then the socialization process during the citizen's development and the day-to-day action of the mature adult, will both be shaped by that ideology, and lead to an acceptance of the status quo.

Let us summarize the argument so far. Through an interrogation of both the material conditions of people and of the ideas that govern how they see themselves and society, the radical view rejects both the internal consistency of traditional pluralist ideas and their correspondence to the actual world of the conscious subject. It therefore builds on an entirely different foundation: a world in which there is a basic structural inequality that is reproduced through generations; in which this inequality is sustained through the ideological apparatus of both the media and the State; in which untheorized facts are not facts at all, since no facts can be perceived except through the apparatus of consciousness which itself is socially constructed and hence imbued with

---

[8] We must be careful of two functionalist errors in our discussion of ideology. The first is to say that, of course we expect accepted ideas to be the ideas of the ruling class. The evidence is that they are still ruling. The second is that once we have identified all sayings and writings within our current society as necessarily ideological, we can dismiss any statements with which we disagree, on the ground that they must by definition be falsely ideological – to be acceptable to the general readership, they have to be.

ideology; in which employees are exploited by the owners of capital as mediated through the control of organizational management; and in which (though we have not discussed this, for lack of space) the instabilities and inherent contradictions of the system lead to recurrent crises that are not aberrations from a basic equilibrium (as most systems theory would suggest) but are an immanent feature of the social, economic and political system.

What are the implications of this for accounting? It renders quite untenable the perception of accounting as a neutral, unbiased source of information. Accounting is provided by some parties for consumption by others. It follows that, consciously or not, the way the information is used and presented will promote the views of the dominant actors in the class struggle in their own interests and on the basis of their own world-views.[9] The information can be used for specifics – to present a picture of profits that suits management in a round of wage bargaining and permits them to argue that a wage increase cannot be afforded; it can also be used in a more general way, as in the case of the value-added statement which is frequently presented in the form of a pie chart to show the employees how much they receive in contrast to the shareholders; and even more generally, by reinforcing the language of profits, retained earnings and dividends, to legitimate the existing social structure by constant repetition (such as the "obvious" statement that dividends have to be paid otherwise new capital will not be forthcoming).

LABOUR PROCESS APPROACHES TO ACCOUNTING AND MANAGEMENT CONTROL

With the completion of this initial structure, we now turn to some specific studies in management accounting and management control. In doing so we find that because of the very nature of the radical position, the subject of the enquiry is quite different.

---

[9] A world-view (sometimes left in the German, *Weltanschauung*) is the way that a person or class of people comes to perceive the nature of the social world as a result of their own particular socialization process. Given the nature of ideology we have described, it follows that (according to the school of thought followed) world-views in class societies are either moulded deterministically as a false consciousness so as to obscure the true nature of the class relationship (ideology as a negative process), or are the necessary constitutive frameworks required to make sense of the world – though still imbued with ideology (ideology as a positive process).

Unlike the traditional and systems positions, it no longer asks about the way control systems can or should operate to ensure the smooth and efficient running of the operation. It asks instead: what is the nature of the employment relation? Who has power in the way this relation operates and the way the management accounting function is implicated in control? And what are the consequences of this?

A helpful starting point is the paper by Hopper, Storey and Willmott (1987). This paper contains two tables which are extremely helpful in clarifying the differences of approach between a radical investigation into the operations of capitalist organizations and the approaches taken by traditional and interactionist approaches (labelled by them "naturalistic" approaches). Their tables have been combined into one in Table 4.1. In the table they consider eight features of management accounting, and the way these are explicated in traditional and interactionist approaches. These leave some questions unanswered (column 4); and the radical (critical) perspective's claims to provide answers to these are outlined in the final two columns.

Hopper, Storey and Willmott call their approach a "labour process approach" (though expressing only qualified satisfaction with the label). The productive organizations of capitalism seek to find and undertake activities that lead to a profitable surplus. Hence the employer, or manager, is faced with the task of organizing the labour process so as to ensure that there is a surplus value above the cost of production. Non-managerial employees have no interest in the work itself and the concomitant success of their employer, since they have been reduced to a commodity (capital is buying from them their labour power, not themselves as whole sentient beings). Thus there is a basic conflict between the worker selling his or her labour power for the highest price and the owner seeking the lowest price so as to maximize surplus value. This disarms any attempt to improve the operation of the workplace by, for example, the common nostrums of human relations thinking such as participation and self-fulfilment through the nature of the job. These cannot resolve conflict which is immanent. Instead they can only forestall it – papering over the cracks or displacing one conflictual arena to another.

Although traditional theory implies that management is driven towards efficiency through the operations of markets, this is not consistent with control of the labour process as it is observed in practice. A telling example is provided by Clawson describing the work of scientific management, the apparent zenith of capitalistic expropriation:

The "efficiency experts" responsible for introducing systems of scientific management at Watertown Arsenal simultaneously made changes to the accounting systems, making it impossible to ascertain the managerial costs associated with the changes either for specific departments, or to evaluate the efficiency gains or otherwise for the schemes as a whole.

                                        (Clawson, 1980, p. 450)

This reinforces an earlier point also taken from Clawson. He argued that in the nineteenth century the management of large organizations moved from internal subcontracting (in the early days of factories the owners permitted foremen to hire their own labour and pay them themselves) to totalizing hierarchies. They did so not because these were more efficient but because they provided a better means of controlling the workforce and making its activities transparent through the cost accounting systems that grew up. Accounting, in other words, was not a neutral source of information that led to the socially-desirable goal of efficiency, but a system to reinforce the power of the owners over their employees by permitting control over every aspect of their work through the minutiae of cost analysis. In this way, knowledge of the financial aspects of the organization moved upwards, away from those involved in everyday production to those at the top who controlled them.[10]

The study by Ogden and Bougen (1985) into the disclosure of information to trade unions makes a point which we referred to in Chapter 1 and which is implicit in the title of this chapter: that conventional stories about industrial relations are told from the point of view of management.[11] Management, representing the owners, has captured not just the ear of the State, dedicated to maintaining the system in which owners continue to control and managers continue to manage, but has also captured the attention of the consultants and academics who write about "organizational

---

[10] An interesting and recent confirmation of this may be found (though not interpreted this way) in Earl and Hopwood (1980). They document the way that black books and other unofficial media were kept by lower managers, generally in preference to the official information systems. When they presented the results of the research, senior management wanted these black books "rooted out", despite the presumption that they permitted the keepers of the black books to undertake their jobs more effectively. The evidence seems to point to the instinctive feeling among top management that overall control dominated any other goal, regardless of the implications for efficiency and effectiveness.

[11] There is an interesting parallel here with the well-known observation that history is a tale told by the victors. More seriously, it echoes our discussion of ideology earlier.

TABLE 4.1 Traditional and interactionist approaches to features of management accounting.

Questions about management accounting	Conventional depictions	Naturalistic depictions
1. What are organizational goals?	Organizational goals represent a congruence of interests	Problematical legitimating devices requiring "negotiation"
2. What is the focus of analysis?	Individuals, sub-units and systems	Social interaction
3. What image of organizational reality is presented?	Organizations characterized by rational and co-operative behaviour	Individuals constantly confronted with uncertainty regarding the actions of others
4. What is management accounting?	A technical and neutral information service for decision-making	A process whereby certain designated actors negotiate shared meanings
5. What does management accounting provide?	A mirror-like objective depiction of reality	A language subjectively created, sustained and modified intersubjectively
6. How is the historical development of accounting explained?	As a result of technical and organizational progress	Historical perspective neglected
7. Whose interests are served by management accounting?	Everyone's interests ultimately served by the prospering of owners and managers, who are treated as synonymous	Relatively open, but economic categories and collectivities not a principal or significant basis of analysis
8. What is the conceptualization of deviance?	Malfunctioning by individuals (either purposefully or not) and defects in administrative systems	Actions understood in the context of the actor's subjective meaning system

Remaining problems	General orientation of the critical perspective	Insights into management accounting from a critical perspective
Neglect of organizational goals as articulations of vested interests	The relationship of formal goals to vested interests and their transformation through resistance	Reified devices that channel and legitimate sectional interests
Neglect of institutional analysis	How management control is shaped by the class structure and the regulation of the State	The role of management accounting in the institutionalized subordination of labour
Inadequate explanation of persistent conflict and the elements of compliance	Conflict derived from resistance arising out of fundamental antagonisms between capital and labour	The organization as a site of class struggle and domination
Inadequate theory of power and control	How controls are conditioned by the powers and demands of the capitalist mode of production	Controls as congeries of devices shaped by and reinforcing the dominant mode of production
The partial and interested language of accounting information	The demystification of overtly neutral language	How accounting language serves and legitimates sectional interests
The absence of a political basis to historical analysis	The provision of a perspective which attends to the role of politico-economic forces in the constitution of accounting practice	Seen to emerge largely in response to crises and opportunities presented by the unfolding contradictory logic of the CMP
Failure to grasp the significance of the class structuring of managerial work	Managers' ambiguous position within the class structure	Accounting, like other forms of control, largely fashioned to meet the perceived interests of capital, though shaped also by the demands of inter-professional competition
Deviance not understood in relation to the basic structures of organizations and society	The labelling of "deviance" in relation to the class interests of the labeller	Deviance arises out of the efforts to secure control over recalcitrant labour

problems" and management accounting systems for control. To take management's perspective becomes "natural" and taken-for-granted. After all, the academic writers are mostly employed by business schools.

When we attempt to tell the story from the employee's point of view, we observe that the workplace is inevitably going to become a contested terrain in which both major parties to the struggle – employer and employee – seek control. We have already seen in the Hopper *et al.* paper how capital has historically recognized control over working practices as crucial. Labour appreciates this too. Thus:

> employers usually want to be able to use their labour forces in as flexible a way as possible as they regard labour as a cost to be minimized and a resource to be manipulated: employees, in turn, want to exert some control over the way they are used to prevent or minimize their insecurity and exploitation.
>
> (Hopper *et al.*, 1987, p. 212)

The means used by management to achieve this control include the technology itself (both control over what capital is purchased but also the threat of displacing the worker with machinery), control over the work process (directing the employee in the way the task is undertaken), the deskilling of the job (since this reduces the market power of the worker with specific required skills and makes labour replaceable) and control over information about the profitability of the individual job. But conflict can be expensive to management: so, to achieve the control it wants, it uses various strategies. These include social conditioning – that is, persuading the employee through controlling the context of the job and media such as company newsletters, that he or she is being consulted and is cared for, and that their interests as an employee are consistent with the interests of the employer. The need for persuasion rather than coercion will vary depending on the external environment; in particular, the extent of unemployment in the economy and hence the alternative opportunities available to the worker who objects to coercion.

Managerial control practice thus tends to be a mixture of coercion and persuasion. Ogden and Bougen's main contribution is then to analyse the provision of accounting information in industrial relations bargaining as part of management's apparatus of the control and dissemination of information in order to achieve managerial ends. They explicitly consider other approaches to the provision of information in the context of employee bargaining, and then present a wholly radical alternative in which "accounting information [is] an ideological mechanism for propagating and reinforcing managerial values and purposes". It is an aspect of language; and a language that is designed to make the organization cohere. Moreover, accounting information specifically can divert attention to financial objectives, and through purporting to be neutral can reinforce the notion of the unity of the organization. They point out that the solution proposed by Lau and Nelson (1981) that union mistrust of management may be dissolved by "the services of an independent accountant as an arbitrator of unbiased information", cannot be sustained since such information cannot be "unbiased".

A later paper by Bougen (1989) takes the above analysis further by presenting a very long case study of the provision of information to employees in the context of a profit-sharing scheme in an innovative British company in the 1920s. He argues that the accounting information is "appropriated, mobilized and strategically coupled to particular priorities for partisan and opportunistic purposes". He points out that the management–labour interaction can sometimes be based on matters susceptible to calculation (like wage rates) and sometimes on more ambiguous matters (like mutual trust and the obligation of employees to do as managers tell them). From this beginning he then considers the way that the "injection" of a calculative method (accounting) into the latter (in this case industrial relations at a time of very high labour unrest) can affect the reproduction of the control relationship between management and labour. The case needs to be read in its entirety for its rich detail; but it demonstrates the strategic and tactical use of information by management as the relationship between the profit-sharing scheme and corporate profits is changed over time; and the way that management can use its authority to make this happen in a situation (a special management–labour committee set up to oversee the scheme and discuss generally the problems of the business) that is supposedly one of mutual determination. Throughout, we find the representatives of labour asking questions which are solidly based in their knowledge of the production processes. But we find that without technical knowledge and control over information their objections, at a time of high unemployment, can be overridden.

Bougen considers the lessons to be learned from a specific case of conscious management–worker relations. Armstrong (1985) draws back to consider the way that accountants have come to positions of power within British industry, and the interrelationship between this and the use of financial information as a control device over labour. He rejects the traditional view that "portrays British capitalism as emerging from darkness into light as the potential of accounting controls gradually dawns on sceptical senior managements". Nor is he satisfied solely with the explanation from recent radical industrial sociologists, which argues that nineteenth century capitalists had to face intensified competition; that they found internal contracting systems to be inadequate to obtain the effort out of the workforce that was needed for them to prosper; that piece-rate payment systems likewise were inadequate because of workers' skills in husbanding their efforts to keep the rates up: and that they therefore turned to accounting systems to aid scientific management in its detailed control over the labour process. Instead, he wishes to complement this with a second strand of argument that draws from the sociology of the professions. Each self-designated profession seeks to protect itself against others for a number of reasons, not the least of which is financial. The work from which he draws takes industrial engineers as its subject and argues that the engineers, in the face of their potential displacement from power by the growth of bureaucratic structures, used scientific management as a means of reasserting their power, since they were best suited to install and administer the techniques it entailed. However, Armstrong points out that, valid though this seems to be, it does not explain the way that accountants rather than engineers have attained dominant positions in UK industry. He therefore analyses the three professions of accountants, engineers and personnel managers, all of whom might legitimately make some claim to providing the control skills necessary to dominate the managerial elite.

Rather than detail his further argument here, it is more appropriate to comment on the way it fits into the themes of this chapter. In our initial exposition we discussed only employer and employee, capital and labour, without any explanation of subsidiary or intermediate classes or groups. Management was, implicitly, and unproblematically, serving the interests of capital (Hopper *et al.* referred to management as "materially privileged wage labour"). To suppose the capitalist world was like this would of course be just as simplistic as was the pre-agency theory framework of finance, in which managers automatically, unquestioningly and selflessly made decisions that were best for shareholders. We need to take account of the many parties involved, and intra-class conflict among self-defined groups is as much to be expected as (though different in nature from) inter-class conflict. It is this that

Armstrong presents to us.[12] Capitalist society takes as its foundation the necessity for each person without property to sell his or her labour power, calling it a labour market. Thus the conflict arises not from basic human nature (itself a highly questionable expression) but from the design of the social system itself. In a society predicated on struggle for economic resources, a residual outcome will be competition among occupational groups to take what they can from the stock arising from the production of surplus value. Hence just as we introduced Armstrong as "drawing back" from the detail of Bougen, so we might say he introduces issues not relevant to Bougen, whose case focused specifically on a committee representing labour and management, the latter as agents for capital.

ACCOUNTING, LANGUAGE AND IDEOLOGY

We turn now to the second strand of radical argument in the management control literature. This emphasizes the way accounting is socially constructed based upon prevailing social ideology. In outlining this it is as well to begin by pointing to the superficial similarities and fundamental differences between this and the interactionism of Chapter 3. In that chapter we emphasized the way the social world is constructed by individuals through their interaction, and that the result was essentially a negotiated social world. This did not deny notions of social

---

[12] It is interesting to note that there are clear parallels between his radical analysis of inter-professional contests for power and financial reward and those of libertarian theory. The latter, based on individualist liberal philosophy, also depicts the profession as seeking to maximize its power, prestige and wealth (subsumed under the utility of its members) through the various strategies at its disposal, such as the creation of barriers to entry through an examination system and a period of apprenticeship (known to UK accountants as a training contract). The two approaches are nevertheless fundamentally different. The one treats the conflict within the historical structure of class society and situates it within the broader base of class conflict (as Armstrong is concerned with the struggle to gain power within the class structure of the individual firm). The struggle is, in other words, societally located. The other, founded in economic reductionism, takes the group as the vehicle for individual utility maximization, and implicitly transcends the relations of production. Traditional theory makes no mention of the basic structure of society (feudal, capitalist, etc.). The assumptions are therefore always implicit. Generally however it seems to suppose (a) that capitalist society is so natural that its existence need not be mentioned and/or (b) because human nature is what it is (individualist and selfish), what happens in one mode of production would also take place in any other epoch.

structure as such; for instance, Berger and Luckmann observed that "The social reality of everyday life is thus apprehended in a continuum of typifications . . . Social structure is the sum of these typifications and the recurrent patterns of interactions established by means of them." All the same, the starting point was reductionist: the *individual* negotiating an understanding. Radical thought acknowledges that the social world is a construction, and that people make their world; but crucially, it notes that their consciousness is constructed by their material conditions and the ideological apparatus of the age. For some the emphasis is very much on material conditions and the stage of technological progress (the "forces of production"). Clear traces of this are to be found in Bougen's study. For others the emphasis is on the interweaving of thought and material conditions: and particularly, on the dominance of the ideological apparatus in reproducing the structures of capitalism. It is on this that we now concentrate.

Ideology has been treated in many different ways. A clear and beautifully succinct introduction to this is to be found in Larrain (1979). He remarks that ideology may have:

> a negative or positive meaning. On the one hand, ideology may be conceived in eminently negative terms as a critical concept which means a form of false consciousness or necessary deception which somehow distorts men's understanding of social reality: the cognitive value of ideas affected by ideology is called in question. On the other hand, the concept of ideology may be conceived in positive terms as the expression of the world-view of a class. To this extent one can talk of "ideologies", in plural, as the opinions, theories and attitudes formed within a class in order to defend and promote its interests. The cognitive value of ideological ideas is, therefore, set aside as a different problem.
>
> (Larrain, 1979, pp. 13–14)

He goes on to three more distinctions: ideology as subjective (a deformity of consciousness that cannot grasp reality as it is) or objective (reality itself creating the deception); ideology as either particular (some things may be ideological, some can be ideology-free) or general (at the cultural level of society all is inevitably ideologically constructed); and ideology as either the antithesis of science (it involves preconceptions or irrationalities) or coexisting with science (each intertwined as the world-view of a particular class).

In an early and now classic paper, Tinker, Merino and Neimark (1982) critique the claims of positive accounting theory and its adjunct empirical theorizing to be value-free. As evidence they trace the history of the value concept in economic thought, demonstrating its reliance on the societal context in which economics' supposedly value-free and scientific ideas arose. Positive accounting theory, they are saying, has no more claim to be a truth that transcends the material conditions of its genesis than any of these others, including the neoclassical economic paradigm in which agency theory and positive accounting theory have their roots. From our viewpoint, we may concentrate on two features of the paper: first, Tinker *et al.*'s account of a method to fruitfully replace empiricism,[13] and second, the siting of their understanding of ideology within the field delineated above by Larrain. This latter will help us better understand the paper to which we shall then turn, by Neimark and Tinker (1986).

The starting point for their critique of positive accounting differs from our starting point earlier in the chapter. It is that positive accounting theory requires that there should be a possibility of value-free, neutral, social research. This is grounded in a realist philosophy that contends that "reality objectively exists 'out there'" independently of our senses: and hence that different observers should perceive a given phenomenon in the same way. This is challenged by Tinker *et al.*, mainly on the grounds that many of the phenomena treated by positive theory are not available to the senses, and hence cannot be conceived as objective. For instance, they say, "Can we touch an equilibrium . . . or smell an income number and verify their character and existence in the same way that we can (say) with an element or a sulphur crystal?" They couple this with a second criticism: that the choice of phenomenon is inevitably value-laden and hence governs "what is discovered"; and point out the researchers' values that lead modern security price research to start with the "effects" of accounting numbers and transform them into "security price effects" with scarcely a murmur of concern. Crucially, they develop this thesis to argue that there can be no value-free observation or value-free theorizing. The alternative method of enquiry they call historical materialism.[14] This

> contends that knowledge of the world is as much an invention as it is a discovery. "Facts" never speak for themselves and therefore

---

[13] We may conflate empiricism and positive theory here, since empiricist researchers tend to espouse positivist tenets (which does not imply that they accept the emphasis of the accounting choice literature).

[14] This expression has become common among Marxists, though Marx never used it.

consulting the "facts" about reality is never a sufficient explanation as to how we come to know what we know . . . Materialist philosophy differs fundamentally from Realism in that it recognizes that "theory" may come to form part of the reality that the theory purports to describe.

(Tinker, Merino and Neimark, 1982, p. 172)

As an example from management accounting they indicate that

budgets are not merely "best estimates" of what will happen: they are also targets used to motivate managers to adopt particular courses of action . . . In this respect, it is not the forecasting ability of a budget that is important, rather it is the desirability of the situation that it helps create.

(Tinker, Merino and Neimark, 1982, p. 173)

As a result, the subject–object split is illusory: and if we cannot clearly distinguish the subject (observer) from the object (thing observed), then the theorizing has to take this interpenetration into account.

The reader who seeks "the method of historical materialism" to replace "the method of positive research" will at this point be disappointed, because the authors do not provide one. But to seek this is to misunderstand what is happening here. Tinker *et al.* are not suggesting one empirical method as being better than another empirical method; we are not facing a statistical problem. Rather, it is a means of making sense of the world that interrogates the "facts" rather than taking them as given, recognizing both their value-ladenness and their interrelation *as* facts with the theories that attempt to understand them. Facts are historically produced and identified. Part of the lesson here is that we cannot separate philosophy and method any more than we can separate subject and object. Interpreting the results of the method must, through the arguments of the philosophical underpinnings, be undertaken differently and in the context of the *meaning* of "the facts".

Apart from its appearance in the title, the term "ideology" is not commonly employed in Tinker *et al.*'s paper. Nevertheless it imbues the argument. What, then, is the implicit conception of ideology within the series of possibilities outlined by Larrain? Firstly, it appears to be a positive understanding of ideology: enquiring subjects come to understand their worlds through their socially-conditioned consciousness. There is no sign here of a simplistic negative conception of dominant ideology. Second, my reading of Tinker *et al.* suggests to me that they see ideology as objective rather than subjective: that is, the determining feature lies in the nature of reality, rather than in the perceptual apparatus of the individual consciousness. Third, it is not possible to distinguish whether or not they see ideology as permeating the whole cultural sphere, since they are concerned only with a part of it (the economic-accounting sphere): but it is probable that they do. Finally, they appear to see ideology and science as antithetical: for they suggest a "better" scientific means of apprehending a truth that, by being self-conscious about the theory-laden nature of reality, can transcend the limitations of empiricism.

Turning now to a specific radical research study as it applies to management control, we briefly consider Neimark and Tinker (1986). Their study is grounded in the international strategies of the General Motors Corporation in the USA over a period of sixty years. It attacks conventional views that seek to understand the operations of management control (giving particular attention to transaction cost theory, agency theory, inducement-contribution theory and contingency approaches), arguing that these are themselves culture-bound and take no account of the dynamics of social development. The framework suggested in its stead is a *dialectical* approach to social analysis.

This is said to have four characteristics: first, the pervasiveness of social change; second, the importance of contradictions[15] in driving that social change; third, the tightly-knit interdependence of organization and environment, where they form "an internally related totality"; and fourth, the importance of self-awareness on the part of the observer in understanding social change (the academic researcher is neither independent nor ineffectual).

In the place of traditional control models, Neimark and Tinker offer an understanding that begins from social ideology. This leads managements to perceive their problem as twofold: satisfying the need for productivity, and ensuring the goods thus produced can be sold. Each of these features requires a supportive institutional framework – for example, state-supported education to improve the productivity of the workforce, and a legal framework to enforce sales contracts. Social institutions in turn are not automatic providers of these benefits. Business organizations seek proactively

---

[15] Contradictions in a social system are an inevitable part of the struggle among parties. The tensions within capitalism result in features that "pull both ways at once". Neimark and Tinker themselves offer the example of the wages paid to labour: capital wishes at one and the same time to make them low (so as to maximize the surplus value appropriated by capital), and yet to make them high (so as to provide a market for the goods and services produced).

to change the institutional framework. Overlaid on top of this is the social conflict over the distribution of the surplus from production. Hence all these features can only be understood in terms of the social ideology of the age, which supports and promotes the economic and social system. Crucially, they argue, the nature of these features will change over time, a point overlooked by traditional management control theory. They support this with an analysis of General Motors' annual reports, which they periodize into (a) the 1920s–30s; (b) 1946–65; (c) 1966 to the present. They argue that both the importance of internationalization as a strategy and the type of strategy used has changed over time. The study is also able to explain why actions may sometimes be in the interest of capital as a whole, and at other times of individual capitals only (when they are locked in international competition). Thus their extensive empirical study of the control strategy of GM adds both the historical dimension missing from conventional research, and a conception of the interpenetration of GM and its environments; and since the study focuses on annual reports, the ideology contained in those reports is seen as significant in sustaining the matrix of ideology in US capitalist society more broadly.

CONCLUSION

A radical/critical literature in management accounting has arisen only over the past ten years (in contrast to other areas of social science where there is a long and honourable history). It questions not the minutiae of traditional management accounting, but rather the social framework within which it tacitly operates. The result is that the problems addressed are quite different from conventional textbook problems, they are viewed in a different social context, and they lead to quite different conclusions because they are viewed from quite a different perspective. Traditional theorists seek to improve practice through techniques. Systems theorists seek improvement through a recognition of the totality and interrelations within the organizational system. Many interactionists may see their task as particularistic observation for *Verstehen*, hence leading to improvement in calculative operations. All this is inverted by radical theory. But radical theory still, however tacitly, has a vision of some things that are fundamentally wrong and might be changed. As we proceed into the next chapter we find that such a vision has been abandoned not by default, but quite deliberately. If radical theory shakes the ground under our feet, poststructuralism removes the ground altogether, offering no obvious replacement.

DISCUSSION QUESTIONS

1. Distinguish between conceptions of industrial society and capitalist society. How is this distinction important in understanding the role of a management accounting system?
2. What do we mean by the relations of production? How are these important to our understanding of the role of management accounting in an organization?
3. "Management accounting is necessary to keep costs under control. If this is not achieved, a company will fail in the market." Do you agree? Is this the only explanation of the growth of management accounting in industry?
4. Can management accounting be a neutral mechanism?
5. Why is an understanding of the nature and role of the State important to understanding how management control systems have flourished?
6. "Co-operatives are socialistic enterprises. But you still find they have cost accounting systems, just like any privately-owned company. This shows that management accounting is inescapable for good management." Do you agree with the statement?
7. Consider the relationship between scientific management and cost control techniques. How have these been affected by historical circumstances?
8. Are systems theory and radical theory mutually incompatible in all respects?

5

Universal Abandon

In Gottfried's poem Tristan goes of his own accord to Ireland to seek healing of Iseut. He arrives at the port of Develin (Dublin), whence he is taken to the court. Knowing that, as the slayer of Morholt, he is taking his life in his hands, he tells Iseut that his name is Tantris. This was a touch that would delight the imagination of the Middle Ages, which always admired cunning in the outwitting of an enemy. To us, of course, it is charmingly naive; it is very much as if a modern novelist were to ask us to believe that Mr Winston Churchill managed to maintain himself for some weeks in the Cabinet councils of the Nazi party by calling himself Chinston Wurchill. Still, there it is in the legend, and an important feature of it; and we have to accept it in the spirit in which it is offered.

– Ernest Newman, *Wagner Nights*

One thing that we have observed in the past three chapters is that accounting is defined very differently in each; that different aspects of accounting are given prominence in each; and that they treat accounting differently as a result. Once again we find a new entry point to accounting in this chapter: and to find how it arises we have to ask some fairly fundamental questions.

Just as we explained how radical research would not take as its starting point notions such as managerial efficiency of management accounting systems, neither should we expect that from the research in this chapter, either. In that sense it has something in common with Chapter 4. But its chief distinguishing feature from

Chapter 4 is that radical research has been quite *unitary* (at least in the philosophy behind any given paper). There is a notion of purposiveness, and radical research has this in common with traditional research. Each envisages improvement; for traditional theory, this means improvement in techniques and efficiency; for radical theory, it means transformations in social relations through changes in social structures. But we now enter a world where the very idea of improvement of the human condition through the exploration of knowledge is rendered problematic, and the unitary nature of a knowledge claim or research process is also immanently questioned. And as we get to the later part of the chapter, we find approaches that raise even more fundamental doubts.

As we have noted previously, traditional "common sense" arises mainly from English philosophical schools, with strong influence particularly from Hobbes and Locke. Chapters 2 to 4 relied in the main on German thinkers: Schleiermacher, Dilthey, Husserl, Schutz, Hegel and Marx. With this chapter we also find a national focus in its antecedents, and if anything, these are even more closely focused on one country as a source – France. Those on whom we shall focus in this chapter – Foucault and Derrida – are French and working within a long-standing tradition in that country, albeit one that has seen many convolutions.[1]

Accounting research has, then, picked up on a very healthy tradition here, and one that is still very much alive (Derrida and others such as Deleuze, Latour and Baudrillard are all living at the time of writing, and Foucault died only in 1983). One matter may be worthy of mention in these opening remarks. As with so many of the other thinkers considered in this book, who have been translated across to accounting, accounting was never their principal concern; and no doubt they would have (initially at least) been astonished at the way they have attracted attention from accounting scholars. In the case of the writers we are concerned with here, an especially interesting feature is that they have moved away, in their central focus, from labour and production. This would seem to be the natural focus for management accounting, since it is concerned with the regulation of labour practices in the workplace. Both traditional and radical theorists found this aspect central. Yet, as Poster has pointed out, Foucault's work, to which we shall turn first,

---

[1] The most obvious exception to this is the line that can be traced from Nietzsche and Heidegger to Foucault and Derrida, as well as the obvious comment that all such theory inevitably has strong traces of a dialogue with Marx. A broad discussion of these issues, however, would take us beyond our remit.

analyses spaces outside of labour – asylums, clinics, prisons, schoolrooms, and the arenas of sexuality. In these social loci Foucault finds sources of radicality that are not theorized by Marx and the Marxists.

(Poster, 1979, p. 156)

In a different vein, Baudrillard also in his early work repudiated the focus of Marx on labour, arguing that Marx had fallen into the same trap as bourgeois theory, in reducing the richness of living subjects to their labour.

Yet using these frameworks, accounting theorists have contributed in a major way to the literature. This raises therefore a first point of the freshness that this school of thought brings: it emancipates us from an understanding of accounting discourse as being solely that concerned with production and labour, and thus emphasizes that more is going on in the accounting arena than is envisaged in the more obviously-focused texts.

It is also as well to raise the difficulty of the language used by these thinkers at this stage. It is inevitable that the language of social theory, particularly that summarized in Chapters 4 and 5, has been and will be very complex. This is because the phenomena with which we are concerned are themselves complex and are not amenable to simple exposition. This problem is a very common one in the physical sciences and mathematics, where, for example the theories of modern particle physics can only be expressed satisfactorily in mathematics – which is why so many physicists are opposed to popularizations of, say, quantum mechanics. Even at the level of elementary mathematics it is difficult to express in words

$$\int_{\frac{1}{4}}^{\frac{1}{2}} \sin^3 2x \cos^2 x \, dx$$

(Try it!) In the social sciences the difficulties are far greater because we have no equivalent of mathematical notation, given the imprecision of the terms with which we work. Thus we are using words to express something that can barely be expressed, and using words never designed for the kinds of concepts involved. Reading the originals can therefore be daunting. In what follows, I have tried to use simple language so far as possible. This means I shall inevitably oversimplify and (if this concept is meaningful) distort. That is a price we shall have to pay: but hopefully the gain is access into the literature itself. However, a final warning might be: if you think what you read here is obvious or clear, you have probably not understood it!

One final comment is in order. With the exception of Marx, no single thinker we have discussed up to now has on his own been so deeply influential on social and organizational aspects of management accounting that we needed to concentrate in great detail on their work. Normally they worked within schools of thought: and it was the schools of thought rather than individuals that influenced accounting. That is not true of those in this chapter, especially Foucault. A recent survey of writers quoted found him to be, for the two years that were analysed, the ninth most frequently cited author in the accounting literature. We must, therefore, accord Foucault an especially prominent place in the book. The reason is, simply, that the way he has been used by accounting researchers relies very much on his specific methodological framework; and relies too (and this is intertwined) on the types of social practices he considered in his historical studies. We shall thus begin with a brief explanation of who Foucault was and the types of study he undertook, only then moving on to the characteristic features of his work, before seeing how he has influenced management accounting research.

MICHEL FOUCAULT

Michel Foucault was born in 1926. His first book was published in 1954; however, the string of works for which he is best known began with *Folie et Déraison–Histoire de la Folie à l'âge classique* in 1961, later amended and translated as *Madness and Civilization*. Since then his book-length work has included (English titles given here only, but with the dates being those of the original French publication) *The Birth of the Clinic* (1963); *The Order of Things* (1966); *The Archaeology of Knowledge* (1969); *Discipline and Punish* (1975); and *History of Sexuality* Vol. 1 (1976). The last-named was intended to be the first of six volumes in all; a further three volumes were published, but his untimely death in 1983 prevented completion of the series. In addition, a key text is *Power/Knowledge* (1980), which reproduces a number of interviews with Foucault between 1972 and 1977; this has been invaluable to commentators in clarifying his (particularly methodological) views. Throughout his life Foucault was also politically engaged (for instance, in the prison reform movement) and was frequently called on to express opinions on the issues of the day on French television.[2]

---

[2] French television seeks the political judgements of intellectuals. In Britain we evince more interest in the political inclinations of actors and singers. This illustrates the gulf that has always separated France and Britain.

A perusal of these titles is enlightening. They cover a wide range; they are mainly historical studies of extreme particularity; and they also include methodological studies. The range we see here explains how Ian Hacking (1986) can wryly observe that "'key words' in Foucault's work would be, for example: Labour, Language, Life, Madness, Masturbation, Medicine, Military, Nietzsche, Prison, Psychiatry, Quixote, Sade, and Sex." However, we cannot properly understand the topics that Foucault focused on without first understanding his method, which is intertwined with his view of the nature of enquiry and truth. Only then is it possible to see why he considered the topics that he did, and likewise to understand how they might impact on accounting research.

Archaeology and genealogy

Foucault's unusual approach to historical knowledge is in fact two methods: archaeology and genealogy; the second supplanted the first from *Discipline and Punish* onwards. However, it could be argued that genealogy in many ways *incorporates* archaeology, and, indeed, that elements of genealogy were always implicit in archaeology (cf. Dreyfus and Rabinow, 1982, p. 104). It is genealogy that is usually referred to in accounting research. Nevertheless, we shall begin our investigation with archaeology. So, what does Foucault mean by archaeology as a method towards truth?

Davidson (1986) argues that Foucault put it at its most succinct in the following words: "'Truth' is to be understood as a system of ordered procedures for the production, regulation, distribution, circulation and operation of statements" (Foucault, 1980, p. 133).[3] This should come as a shock. It is quite different from the usual Anglo-Saxon approach to truth – that it constitutes some kind of correspondence to "the facts", so that a true statement correctly represents what is. The problem of ideology rendered the latter problematic, as we saw in the last chapter. But Foucault has no faith in the concept of ideology either, as an all-embracing concept masking the truth. Thus he concentrates on a particular system of thought. Systems of thought vary through the ages. He wishes to bypass any suggestion that there might be a necessary connection

---

[3] We use quotations quite extensively in this chapter. This is because the authors considered eschew interpretation, which means that any form of words we may use as paraphrases of the authors' views could be summarily rejected. The original, wherever possible, is therefore crucial.

between different ages, and certainly to deny that there might be a truth that transcends these different periods. It is in this connection that he has been described as a philosopher of discontinuity (though he did not like this description, which we shall return to later). If there is no transcendental truth, there can only be a localized truth within a particular discourse which, in turn, constitutes and is constituted by discursive practices in a particular historical period.

The archaeological method, then, examines discursive practices.[4] Moreover, it does so in terms of the system of thought at the time. The result of this is that it does not, as traditional histories do, concentrate on what seems important to us through twentieth-century eyes. It looks at what was important as seen at the time. As a result, it "is a fascinating recovery of all the discards and failures and forgotten areas of human thought" (Harland, 1987, p. 102). In traditional accounting historiography, for instance, what seem important are the early origins of double entry, or the first signs of overhead allocation, because these constitute our current practices. But to privilege these, Foucault would, I think, say, is to distort the matrix of social and calculative practices at the time of their "emergence", and therefore to miss the point of how they did in fact emerge.

This results in an inversion. Here is Foucault discussing the advent of modern medical science:

> It is as if for the first time for thousands of years, doctors, free at last of theories and chimeras, agreed to approach the object of their experience with the purity of an unprejudiced gaze. But the analysis must be turned around: it is the forms of visibility that have changed; the new medical spirit . . . is nothing more than a syntactical reorganization of disease in which the limits of the visible and invisible follow a new pattern.
>
> (Foucault, 1963, p. 195)

---

[4] It may not be too much of an exaggeration to say that most systems of understanding in the human sciences have concentrated on *consciousness* as their starting point. In this century the focus has switched to *language,* since we are constituted by language, and thus in this sense language comes prior to consciousness. Traditional and systems theories are oblivious to the language problem; interpretation is still more concerned with the way people understand each other as people than in understanding how they frame their communications; radical theory has more recently incorporated linguistic analysis, but does not have its roots therein. The traditions within which Foucault developed included a heavy reliance on structuralism, which we shall consider later; and structuralism is normally traced back to Saussurean linguistics.

Thus we cannot understand truth separate from the discourses that take place:

> his method is to ask what rules permit certain statements to be made; what rules order these statements; what rules permit us to identify some statements as true and some as false; what rules allow the construction of a map, model or classificatory system; what rules allow us to identify certain individuals as authors; and what rules are revealed when an object of discourse is modified or transformed.
>
> (Philp, 1985, p. 69)

However, for Foucault, genealogy superseded archaeology. The key addition was his concern with power. Genealogy understands truth in terms of power: as Davidson puts it:

> Genealogy . . . has a wider scope than archaeology. Its central area of focus is the mutual relations between systems of truth and modalities of power, the way in which there is a "political regime" of the production of truth . . .
>
> (Davidson, 1986, p. 224)

He quotes the synoptic comment from Foucault:

> "Truth" is linked in a circular relation with systems of power which produce and sustain it, and to effects of power which it induces and which extend it. A "regime" of truth.

Foucault sometimes seems to imply that he has left discursive forms behind in this:

> one's point of reference should not be to the great model of language (*langue*) and signs, but to that of war and battle. The history which bears and determines us has the form of a war rather than that of a language: relations of power, not relations of meaning.
>
> (Foucault, 1980, p. 114)

This brings us to a central issue in Foucault's thought, reflected in the title of the book from which the above quotation is taken, *Power/Knowledge* (more allusive in the French original, *pouvoir/savoir*). In his historical studies, particularly the last two, Foucault is concerned with the way in which regimes of power have grown and have been sustained through disciplinary mechanisms and the institution of norms for human behaviour. He comments how "It was Nietzsche who specified the power relation as the general focus, shall we say, of philosophical discourse – whereas for Marx it was the production relation"

(Foucault, 1980, pp. 53–4). The result of these disciplinary practices are what he calls "totalizing discourses". He wishes to subvert these, and to rediscover the fragmented knowledges that were suppressed through these practices. In this sense Foucault's project was an enabling one for resistance, although this is frequently unclear from the accounting use of his work (cf. Moore, 1991). Foucault sees power as diffused, in the sense that it infuses all discourse and action. "Power operates to constrain or otherwise direct action in areas where there are a number of possible courses of action open to the agents in question." But contrary to the liberal view that power is essentially a force which impedes the development of knowledge by repression and constraint, Foucault argues that power is an integral component in the production of truth: "Truth isn't outside power, or lacking in power . . . Truth is a thing of this world: it is produced only by virtue of multiple forms of constraint. And it induces the regular effects of power" (Foucault, 1980, p. 131).

Since this may still be confusing, we might helpfully look to Richard Rorty's understanding of what Foucault is claiming by contrasting it with other theories of knowledge. He says he will consider three: the Cartesian, the Hegelian, and the Foucauldian.

The Cartesian view of knowledge, Rorty suggests, is normal academic epistemology. The hard sciences are objective, mature and rational. The moral sciences are not – their discourses may not count as knowledge. But if we see how the hard sciences succeed we can apply this insight to the *Geisteswissenschaften*. "Rational inquiry, the Cartesian says, is the process of insuring that representations correspond to reality – so a fixed reality means a fixed method" (Rorty, 1986, p. 44). This is of course the method we find in traditional management accounting research. It is reassuringly familiar.

The Hegelian attitude says that rationality must be seen both sociologically and historically. It sees knowledge as progressing; but it is our culture that progresses, rather than our ability to fit representations to an ahistorical reality. We replace the "correspondence to reality" with a "progress of thought" (ibid., p. 44). The developments of scientific, social and moral progress are *all* dialectical. The radical view we have already outlined is broadly in this tradition.

Rorty suggests that Foucault's approach falls into neither of these categories, although it is tempting to see him as being a Hegelian. Rather he is Nietzschean. He sees both the Hegelian and the Cartesian positions as essentially similar and wrongheaded, because "both. . .say something general and optimistic about the way things have been going for the past few centuries", whereas "Foucault's Nietzschean attitude towards the idea of epistemology is that there is *nothing* optimistic to say. . . . The Nietzschean wants to *abandon* the striving for objectivity" (ibid., p. 46). Thus "to see Foucault as a Nietzschean enemy of historicism rather than as one more historicist enemy of Cartesianism, we need to see him as trying to write history in a way which will destroy the notion of historical progress", because his aim is to "introduce into the very roots of thought" the notions of "chance, discontinuity and materiality". However here we may observe the playful philosopher in Foucault (playfulness is not an accusation; it may be intrinsic to certain kinds of poststructuralism and, indeed, may be essential as a counterweight to the linearity of positivism). In an interview, Foucault remarked that a dictionary described Foucault as "a philosopher who founds his theory of history on discontinuity": "That leaves me flabbergasted" (Foucault, 1980, p. 111). He later made his position more clear:

> My problem was not at all to say "*Voilà*, long live discontinuity, we are in the discontinuous and a good thing too" but to pose the question "How is it that at certain moments and in certain orders of knowledge, there are these sudden take-offs, these hastenings of evolution, these transformations which fail to correspond to the calm, continuist image that is normally accredited?"
>
> (p. 112)

It is at this point that the reader can see why Foucault is so revolutionary in comparison to the other thinkers and schools of thought which we have considered. The Nietzschean turn inverts what we may normally think of as the task of the academic analyst, to make sense of a complex world for us. This must rely on a hope that there is a sense that we can make of this world. Foucault, it seems, wishes to take that hope away from us. This is not to say, of course, that he does not have many insights to offer. He has many, because his whole method revolves around the constant alighting upon facts. And here again we can see a distinction between Foucault and the radical of Chapter 4 (though many would see Foucault as a very different kind of radical, and I would not disagree with that – we just have problems of boxing people into categories, and finding the right language in any given case). The latter is cautious of facts because they are value-laden in an ideological world. Foucault is certainly cautious about interpreting facts: but he has no hesitation in presenting them in abundance.

We may perhaps make one more point on the subject of genealogy. This is well expressed in an accounting paper by Miller and Napier (1990). Traditional accounting historical research, they point out, is concerned with the search for origins. It asks how a certain historical feature arose. But Foucault rejects this because, in rejecting the idea of the *essence* of a feature that is to be analysed, it is also necessary to reject its singular emergence as a thing. Instead of this, they say, "genealogy seeks to demonstrate that the essence or secret of things was fabricated in a piecemeal fashion from disparate components, only achieving consummate form in the self-evidence of the present" (Miller and Napier, 1990, p. 15).

Let us put this another way. What we suppose we have in traditional accounting history is something that has an essence: for instance, cost accounting. This changes and develops over time, improving between, say, the eighteenth and twentieth centuries. Yet it is still a thing called cost accounting. Genealogy rejects the idea that we can just specify something like cost accounting as if it has such an essence that could be traced. What happens at any particular time as a calculative method (which is what cost accounting is) can be understood through its links to other practices at that time. At another time, in another system of thought, there will be a different set of constituents. Each of these can be spoken of. But it is mistaken to suppose that they relate to the same thing; for genealogy rejects the idea of progress that transcends historical periods. It "seeks to trace the relations that link practices together into a delicate tracery or filigree".

Foucault's subject-matter

We have already looked at the titles of Foucault's books and a list of his interests. Now we can turn briefly to an example of the topics with which his historical work was concerned. We shall take the first study that was recognizably infused with the genealogical method: his study of punishment and incarceration, *Discipline and Punish: the Birth of the Prison*. It is concerned with a feature we referred to earlier, namely, regimes of power as means of control.

Genealogy is concerned with the relationship between power, knowledge and the body in modern society (Dreyfus and Rabinow, 1982): this is epitomized in the practices of punishment in society. Foucault opens with a horrific description of the public torture and execution of a man guilty of regicide (don't read it straight after lunch); without any transitional explanation the text switches straight to the timetable of rules for daily routine in a nineteenth-century prison. The two episodes are eighty years apart. They are juxtaposed to raise questions about the change from visible punishment to the hidden but all-embracing regimen of the prison. This latter, in turn, may illustrate what has happened more generally in society over the past 200 years. Through the close specification of methods of ordering prisons and prisoners, and through the close observation of the activities of those prisoners, at its most idealized in Jeremy Bentham's plan for a Panopticon,[5] it may be seen as a microcosm of the increased control under which the person has been placed since that time. It is here that we can see how Foucault's method is crucial to his conclusions.

The decisive section of *Discipline and Punish* is Part 3: Discipline. Here Foucault has trawled through historical archives to find the ways people are ordered in so many small ways. Some are obvious, such as judicial procedures that testify as to an accused's mental state. Others are less obvious, such as the way that the working man's cottage has its rooms divided so as to ensure a strict morality. People are registered; files are kept on them; they are subjected to hospital examinations; in institutions such as armies and prisons they are physically regimented into neat lines; in those same institutions there are classification schemes beyond military ranks based on moral behaviour; there is an "accountancy of diseases, cures, deaths, at the level of a hospital, a town, and even . . . the nation" (p. 190). Writing itself serves to control. All these mechanisms, by creating visibility, enhance power over the body. It is by enumerating these small matters, as "lowly", perhaps, as the parish register, that Foucault is able to show a whole disciplinary control mechanism in modern society.

So why does Foucault begin with the regicide's public torture and execution? To emphasize the way that visibilities changed. As Charles Taylor points out,

> For our eyes, the details of the execution of Damiens bespeak gratuitous cruelty, sadism. Foucault shows that they had another reason then. The punishment can be seen as a kind of "liturgy". Human beings are seen as set in a cosmic order, constituted by a

---

[5] This was the ideal prison design (a plan and illustration are included with Foucault's text). It was circular in shape, so that all cells could be viewed from the centre. Prisoners could always be seen; but they would not know when they were being observed, so that the effects of observation were potentially constant. As we shall see later, accounting analysts can use this also as an ideal type for their discussions of Taylorism and the use of cost accounting systems to manifest and reinforce the Taylorist conception of work.

hierarchy of beings which is also a hierarchy of goods. They stand also in a political order, which is related to and in a sense endorsed by the cosmic one. This kind of order is hard to explain in modern terms, because it is not simply an order of things, but an order of meanings. Or to put it in other terms, the order of things which we see around us is thought to reflect or embody an order of Ideas. You can explain the coherence things have in terms of a certain kind of making sense.

(Taylor, 1986, p. 71)

But, more than this, the function of visibility has changed. In the old order there had been a public space in which the majesty of the king dominated, and kept the people in awe. That public show of power gave way to an invisible network of ways of scrutinizing the subject. Taylor expresses it elegantly: "The ancients strove to make a few things visible to the many; we try to make many things visible to the few" (ibid., p. 74). Thus there is a whole hierarchical set of disciplinary mechanisms acting on the subject to attain and reproduce order.

Foucault and accounting studies

We have provided quite a lengthy exposition of Foucault's (non-accounting) writings. We have done so with a purpose: to show why and how Foucauldian accounting histories differ so markedly from traditional accounting histories. To show how this has been expressed in accounting scholarship, we now turn to the way in which Foucauldian analysis has been used in management accounting research. We shall consider two studies: Anthony Hopwood, *The Archaeology of Accounting Systems*, and Peter Miller and Ted O'Leary, *Accounting and the Construction of the Governable Person*.[6] There is however a distinction to be drawn between them. The second is explicit in its use of Foucault, and outlines relevant aspects of a Foucauldian method as part of its exposition. Its territory is very much that of *Discipline and Punish* in its concern with control mechanisms. Hopwood, on the other hand, although referencing six of Foucault's books in the bibliography, prefers to distance himself from importing Foucault into accounting, allowing just that the work "reflects his reading of the work of Foucault".[7] As we shall see, while there are clear elements of the

---

[6] Other work using Foucault extensively includes Hoskin and Macve, 1986, 1988, and Loft, 1986.
[7] Personal communication to the author.

method to be found, his work is less concerned with highlighting disciplinary practices as such (although this is not omitted altogether).

The Archaeology of Accounting Systems

This paper consists of a lengthy introduction followed by three cases of particular control practices in organizational settings. The words in the opening paragraph, "[accounting] has been called upon to serve an ever greater variety of different and changing purposes . . . Over time, accounting has been implicated in the creation of very different patterns of organizational segmentation" reflect the genealogical method of linking particular practices to other practices in that time period. Variations of the phrase, repeated in the paper, that "accounting has become what it was not" are, as will now be clear, also a reflection of the discontinuity highlighted by archaeological/genealogical methods. Hopwood insists that his paper is tentative, but suggests that the purpose of the paper is to "illuminate at least some of the pressures and processes involved in accounting change" and that overall he is seeking "a more organizationally grounded and a more dynamic understanding of the accounting craft". There follows a critique of existing understandings of accounting in context; and Hopwood remarks that:

> as a basis for understanding either the process or the consequences of such change, conventional views are severely limited. For rather than providing a history of the emergence of accounting as it now is, they provide the basis for the compilation of a history of inadequacy, ignorance and obsolescence when accounting was not what it should be, peppered with only occasional moments of enlightenment when accounting moved nearer to realizing its potential.
>
> (Hopwood, 1987, p. 211)

When Hopwood turns to the way that accounting helps in constructing a social order, he does then turn to issues of social visibility and discipline, explicitly rejecting understandings of accounting that are solely organizational. Accounting, he suggests,

> is not a passive instrument of technical administration . . . instead its origins are seen to reside in the exercising of social power both within and without the organization. It is seen as being implicated in the forging, indeed the active creation, of a particular regime of economic calculation . . .

> A regime of economic visibility and calculation has positively
> enabled the creation and operation of an organization which
> facilitates the exercising of particular social conceptions of power
> . . . The resultant organizational facts, calculations, schedules and
> plans have positively enabled the construction of a management
> regime abstracted and distanced from the operation of the work
> process itself.
>
> (Hopwood, 1987, p. 213)

The Foucauldian insights are clear here: accounting is wholly
implicated in the creation of structures of surveillance and power
that permit modern management to function at a distance from
the work process itself.

Hopwood's three case studies are of Wedgwood in the late
eighteenth century, and of two anonymous other companies in
recent years. Space precludes any detail here; the reader is
encouraged to consult the original. However a key conclusion we
are to draw is that "what conventionally have been seen to be
the statics of the accounting craft have been seen to be in the
process of changing, becoming thereby, what they were not."

I have argued here that Hopwood's analysis is at heart
Foucauldian, and may be used to illustrate the framework of
Foucault that we have outlined so far in this chapter. However
it is not purely so; a particular difference from the empirical
studies by Foucault is that it shows less interest in tracing what
Miller and Napier called the "filigree" of social practices. The
intersection of practices is present; but they are not, as genealogy
promises they might be, small, many and ultimately accumulative
in their disciplinary power. It need hardly be said that this is not
itself a criticism, since Hopwood assures us he never intended the
study to be Foucauldian as such, and there is no need to impose
on his work a framework which was never intended. Our purpose
has been rather, through showing the *intentions* behind archaeology
and genealogy, to illuminate the backcloth against which Hopwood
is working.

Accounting and the Construction of the Governable Person

Miller and O'Leary's frequently-cited paper focuses on the
development of standard costing and budgeting systems in the
early years of the present century. The core of their argument is
that these accounting changes cannot simply be seen as a rational
development to improve the accuracy and refinement of managerial
information. Rather, they are just one part of a wide-ranging

extension of the apparatus of power during that period. The practices that developed were intended to make the person, that is, the body, more amenable to being managed and controlled. In the case of cost accounting, this meant making visible "crucial aspects of the functioning of the enterprise [such as] questions of wastage and efficiency". This visibility focused on the individual person, by "surrounding the individual at work by a series of norms and standards [so that] the inefficiencies of the person were rendered clearly visible" (p. 239). The shift was from surveillance by the individual boss to surveillance by a whole technical apparatus of rational calculation.

The most obvious development of the kind they are concerned with is the Taylorist apparatus of surveillance and control over all aspects of the individual task: what has now come to be known as work study. But there were a number of other developments at the same time that are identified by Miller and O'Leary. Other mechanisms in society were developing to compare people against specific standards. What was a central theme here was *efficiency*. Efficiency went far beyond the workplace: that was just one arena in which the drive to efficiency was expressed. Other arenas examined by Miller and O'Leary are the whole discourse of national efficiency through, for example, the eugenics movement and the drive for mental hygiene. With the exception of racist writings, today, we simply do not find arguments like those adduced at that time, the stridency of which seems curiously comparable to the physical violence to the body with which Foucault opens *Discipline and Punish*. One writer, we are told, fetchingly wrote of

> our species [as] being propagated and continued increasingly from undersized, street-bred people . . . Spectacled schoolchildren, hungry, strumous, and epileptic [who] grow into consumptive bridegrooms and scrofulous brides.
>
> (Miller and O'Leary, 1987, p. 244)

The answer was eugenics: to sterilize those who were unfit, thus improving the country's breeding stock. This control over the body, far from being the concern of a few, was not just widely advocated but was also practised. There could be fewer better examples of social discipline and control in the Foucauldian sense.

Allied to this was the drive for mental hygiene. Mental disease, especially in the young, had to be prevented: it could lead to "tantrums, stealing, seclusiveness, truancy, cruelty, sensitiveness, restlessness, and fears" (ibid., p. 249). Again there was a widespread move to social intervention over the individual (such as IQ testing).

Thus, Miller and O'Leary conclude, we cannot understand the developments of cost accounting within the workplace purely as technical improvement. It is one among a network of social practices that interwove and interpenetrated each other during the early part of the century. And the way into understanding this network of practices is genealogy.

STRUCTURALISM AND THE OTHER POSTSTRUCTURALISTS

We now turn from Foucault and his major influence on recent accounting thinking. To understand the other writer we shall be considering in this chapter, Jacques Derrida, we need some further introductory comment. The first comment we make is to point out that, strictly, the order of this chapter is rather odd.

Much French thought this century has been dominated by structuralism, deriving from the pioneering work in the field of linguistics by Ferdinand de Saussure. Structuralism has over the past thirty years tended to give way to poststructuralism; and Foucault is generally classified as a poststructuralist. The justification for leaving our brief explanation of structuralism until after we looked at Foucault is that, not only does an understanding of Foucault not need an understanding of structuralism; but also that structuralism *per se* has had no impact on accounting research. This statement has to be tempered immediately however. The *language* of structuralism has indeed permeated many accounting writers, including some of the work of Tinker and his colleagues. But more importantly, we cannot understand other poststructuralists without considering the concepts within which they work and, in particular, the meanings of the signifier–signified–referent triptych.

A further warning is needed as we work our way up to other poststructuralists. Up to now, matters have been relatively simple. Foucault is not easy: but he still appeals to something we can recognize. But we now have to tackle a body of knowledge that is sufficiently complex that, if at the end of my exposition you think you understand on the first reading, then I have probably explained it badly, and you are probably wrong. We begin to leave behind the supposed order of social science and *Wissenschaft*: we enter a world where the roots of knowledge themselves are within the schools of thought immanently challenged, a world where in interviews, writers are at pains to continually deny that they should be understood as saying what the interviewer thought they were saying, while at the same time declining to be any clearer about what they are saying: and doing so not to evade, but as part of the programme itself. Thus they, as well as Foucault, are against interpretation as a programme. But to explain "what they say" means we have to interpret what they say. Since that is denied as a meaningful enterprise, it means, *inter alia*, that my explanation *must* be wrong insofar as it claims to be the authoritative understanding; your understanding is similarly unreliable; and even your understanding of the original works, were you to return to them, would not permit you to map out a coherent picture of the world by the author (who denies himself-herself as author as a meaningful construct). At the limit this seems a student's dream: because the examinee cannot "get it wrong" in answering the question on the poststructuralists. I would not advise a reliance on this as a study strategy, however.

With this warning to worry you, let us begin with structuralism.

STRUCTURALISM[8]

To understand structuralism in social theory, we must go back to its roots in linguistics, in the work of Ferdinand de Saussure (1857–1913). The story is unusual. Saussure was an eminent but otherwise unexceptional linguistic theorist. In the last three years of his working life he was asked to give a course on general linguistics. He did so, but died shortly after and never wrote them up. His students' notes and his own lecture notes were then used as the sources for a book, *Cours de Linguistique Générale,* assembled by two of his colleagues. It is this book that was a landmark in linguistics and set the scene for extensions into philosophy and social theory.

According to Saussure, we must begin with the *system* of words, rather than individual words and sentences. We must understand language as the total system. This he called *langue.* Within this system particular utterances can be made. These he called *parole.* Thus language is not the result of all the sentences ever spoken, but rather the system within which each individual grows up and which defines the boundaries of what they can utter. I can say "the cat sat on the mat" because the system of

---

[8] Part of this section draws on Cooper and Puxty, forthcoming (a).

langue permits it. I cannot say "cat the mat on sat the" because the system does not permit sense to be made of it.

Each of the words I utter has a conventional meaning: that is, it means something because we are all agreed it does. This results from a kind of contract that we engage in with our linguistic environment. We wish to communicate: the language system enables us to do so. But each term we use is arbitrary. The term "dog" might have been "dayg" and still could have meant the same. Indeed to many people the word is not "dog", it is "chien" or "chienne", or "Hund" or "cane". All these words are taken to refer to the idea of dogginess. So Saussure's system is one of signs; and each sign consists of two parts, a *signifier* and a *signified*. In each case here the signified has been the same, the idea of a dog. The signifier has differed, being dog, chien, Hund, etc. So it is the signifier that is arbitrary as a way of expressing the signified. Language is thereby a sign system.

Since these signs are arbitrary, how do we make sense of them? Saussure's answer is fundamental. We can do so because of their difference from other signs. Suppose A has a high-pitched voice. Then the sound uttered when she says "animal" will differ from its sound when B with a gruff voice says "animal". Yet we all understand them to have expressed the same signified. Thus, we cannot depend on the sound. Instead, we depend on the difference from other signifiers: A also says "magnet" in a high-pitched voice; it is the difference between her utterances of "animal" and "magnet" that enables us to tell to what they refer. So language is only meaningful through difference.

The principle of difference extends to signifieds, too. There is thus a space for each signified in a web of signifieds. Each signified has its own conceptual space. Each signified inches out others when a space is required for it. Equally, in the absence of a signified, the conceptual space of signifieds closes in to fill the gaps. However, signifieds are not "things represented by the words": "The concepts are purely differential and defined not by their positive content but negatively by their relations with the other terms of the system. Their most precise characteristic is in being what the others are not" (Saussure, 1974, p. 117). Yet in all of this there is, in the first instance, something that the sign is referring to: the *referent*. Thus, for instance, when uttering the word "blackbird", the signifier is the nine-letter word; the referent is a living creature with black feathers: and the signified is a bird that is not a robin, or a finch, or a crow. Were there to be no signifier "crow", a means would be needed to indicate the physical feathered creature. It is quite possible that the signifier "blackbird" would take its place, but the physical world of referents would not be changed.[9] Anglo-Saxon ideas in philosophy, with which we tend to be imbued as if they were "common sense", treat objects of study as if all that matters are the word (the signifier) and the referent (the thing-in-the-world). Saussure shows how that cannot be sustained, because it collapses the discursive world to one of naming things. The following discussion may make this a little clearer.

As you may by now have inferred, the referent is of little importance to the language system as Saussure outlines it, contrary to what we might expect when we suppose that discourse is "about things". We shall see where this leads us in a moment, when we turn to poststructuralism. However, for the reader who finds this difficult to accept, here is an illustration. In language we wish to make statements about things. We gave as our example the sign and referent "blackbird". The referent here is clear: it has black feathers, flies, and makes an offensive sound. But now consider the sign "true and fair". What is the referent – the "thing" of which we wish to speak when we make statements about accounting practice? There are fewer difficulties with the signified. It is the set of practices that are appropriate under conditions defined by accountants and lawmakers, and can be defined in its difference from, say, bias, fraudulent misstatement, and so on. But it is difficult to *point* to something true and fair, just as it is impossible to point to "a depreciation" or "a provision for doubtful debts" as things in reality separate from the signs, which are of course the numbers on the balance sheet. So perhaps these only exist at the level of the sign? That is, as we shall see, a key element of poststructuralism.

What we have given is, of course, only a bare outline of Saussure's ideas. However it identifies the characteristic that

---

[9] This is a highly simplified account. For example, it omits the many-faceted system of interdependencies such as "wildlife", "natural environment", "carrion", and so on, that interlink with the signifieds discussed. The signifier "crow" would mean something different were the expression "carrion crow" not to exist. To take another example: the imaginary Martian who visited this world and was told that "Genghis Khan" referred to a warrior who lived some centuries ago would not thereby begin to understand the way the concept Genghis Khan actually works in our language. What is more, by taking a very clear pair of referents we may have given the impression that it is just a matter of objects A and B both having the same name. But this is not what is meant. Consider the terms "evident" and "obvious". If "evident" were to be removed from our language, some of its meaning would be taken by "obvious"; but other aspects of its meaning might be taken by, for instance, "apparent".

became so important in other areas of structuralism, namely its universality. All languages have these features. They are an immanent part of human communication. This could then lead to a generalization of structures: perhaps we could also find such structures in literary texts or in social systems? And indeed this is just what structuralist literary theorists, cultural theorists and anthropologists have sought, and the framework within which they have researched. Until the 1950s and 1960s this was a powerful influence.

This breaks down with poststructuralism,[10] to which we now turn. In doing so I shall consider poststructuralism generally without any clear dividing line between the generalities of poststructuralism and the specific work of Derrida.

POSTSTRUCTURALISM

The very term "poststructuralism" is ambiguous. Does it mean "after structuralism" or "beyond structuralism"? The answer is also ambiguous: but that is itself an element in poststructuralist thought. A question that the reader will now be asking is: how do we identify poststructuralism? There is no easy answer, because that would imply an *essence* of the school or object called poststructuralism: and much of poststructuralism is devoted to undermining belief in such essences. We saw this in a fairly mild form in Foucault's archaeology. But there are more far-reaching critiques of object and essence than this.

We saw in Saussure that three elements were mentioned: signifier, signified and referent. We also saw that the referent is somewhat shadowy. If language is not just a matter of naming things, then perhaps it really is something that is prior to material reality, and dominates material reality? Perhaps indeed it comes to *be*, and hence dominate, material reality? This is territory where the poststructuralist is willing to go.

Those with at least a little familiarity with the leading figures in sociology will be aware of the contribution of Durkheim, who pointed out that there are social phenomena that are not centred on individuals but are prior to them. These include, for example, our beliefs about the world. It is more helpful to understand our

---

[10] "Post" in this sense does not mean "after" chronologically, and there have been debates about whether there was poststructuralism before structuralism. We needn't worry about that.

beliefs about the world in terms of the social collectivities that we are born into, than as the result of an individualistic perception. This is really quite different from the Marxist idea of ideology because for Marx, the latter had material roots within his materialist conception of society. But for Durkheim these sets of beliefs themselves dominate the way we should understand society. In the poststructuralist turn, we have to raise serious questions about the role of the referent. We have seen a structuralist system built with little need for the referent. Do we need it at all? What grounds do we have for our faith in the referent? The answer is: very little. We cannot escape the sign. It is immanent to systems of language, and they in turn dominate the way we understand. We do, however, seem to be able to do without the referent. And this, *inter alia*, is what poststructuralists do. For Foucault it is the terms of discourse that are to be interrogated, rather than "what is", whatever that is. And this brings us to the essence of how the sign works. Harland puts this clearly:

> What the Post-Structuralists invoke as an alternative is an even more signish version of the Sign itself. Characteristically, they distinguish between two possible modes of functioning for the Sign. On the one hand, here is the conventional mode where the Sign works rigidly and despotically and predictably. This is the mode that Structuralists and Semioticians analyse. On the other hand, there is an unconventional mode where the Sign works creatively and anarchically and irresponsibly. This is the mode that represents the real being of the Sign. And when we are true to the real being of the Sign, we find that it subverts the socially controlled system of meaning, and, ultimately, socially controlled systems of every kind.
>
> (Harland, 1987, p. 124)

The implications of this last passage are that, under some conditions, the sign becomes the master and not the servant.

Let us go back again to language. The common-sense position in language seems to be to understand it as the expression of the speaker. If the function of language is to communicate, then we might suppose that it must just reflect what somebody wishes to say. In speech we then have the authority of the speaker giving credence to the words as they are spoken. If we do not understand, we may ask the speaker what was meant. This conventional understanding of language is inverted by Derrida. He claims that, first, writing is more central than speech – that is, that the idea of speech can only exist because of the prior idea of writing. Speech is therefore secondary. Since we cannot interrogate the author on all occasions (in the case of writing the author may be dead anyway) we have to rely on the words as the sole basis for action, and not the intentions behind the writing. We can then extend this further: there is no reason why the writer should be accorded any priority in making sense of the words, and we are all active in making sense of those words (see Cooper and Puxty, forthcoming (b) for a fuller exposition of this). In other words, the reader is freed from the tyranny of the writer through the act of reading, and the writer has no basis for correcting the reader ("But this is what I really meant").

Derrida goes beyond this, to decentre the essence of writing itself. We may suppose we can attempt to write in a way devoid of ambiguity. This is mistaken, says Derrida, because all the terms we use are the confluence of matrices of meaning. These networks of meaning are immanent to language, and they deny us the singularity of communication that we wish. Here is Harland, again:

> Similarly with the Greek word "pharmakon" which can mean both "poison" and "remedy". When Plato, in the *Phaedrus*, applies the word to writing, he seems to be condemning writing as a "poison" (at least in the standard French translations). But Derrida opens the word up to its other sense of "remedy", claiming that "the word *pharmakon* is caught up in a chain of significations . . . [which] is not, simply, that of the intentions of an author who goes by the name of Plato". According to Derrida, the Greek language is saying through Plato's text two quite divergent things about writing, simultaneously and undecidably.
>
> (Ibid., p. 132)

Thus the ambiguity is not just accidental, not a "fault of the language". The *langue* that has grown over the years has for very good reasons incorporated this kind of ambiguity. The network of meaning itself undermines any attempt to avoid immanent contradiction. This startling conclusion raises serious questions in our belief in the centrality of meaning. Take, for instance, the expression "standard costing". The term "standard" has many meanings. It is an ideal ("St Francis of Assisi provides a standard by whom all others should be judged"); it is ordinary (standard size eggs rather than large ones); it is normal ("the standard grade in the examination should be attainable by the average student"); and so on. Accounting textbooks find the need to discuss the appropriate standard for standard costing: the language itself will not help them. The result of this is that the author (such as the designer of the system or the book's author) has to try to circumvent by the use of authority what the language will not supply. The language cannot *of itself* explain its own meaning. Indeed, it cannot but lead to conflict as different readers of the system understand it in different ways.

But what we now have is the signifier "standard costing" as a thing: the sign has come into the world and is part of the world, rather than just a communication. The signifier "standard" in turn points to other signifiers ("ideal", "ordinary", "normal") and the result is a network of signifiers that has grown to become a proliferation of signifiers. We have a chain of referentiality that cannot be stopped.

What should now become clear is how far we have come from our structuralist starting point in which the signifier was just a way of indicating through the mechanism of an arbitrary sign. That sign has now come to dominate (but perhaps only in modern society – this point is open to dispute). The sign is the reality: there is no space for suggesting any other reality. Thus when we argue over what the standard in standard costing is, or the apportionment basis for overheads, or the order in which to perform step-down apportionment, we can have no recourse to "the real" beyond the signs of the costing system itself. This may, perhaps, explain rather better than current technical attempts why there is no unchallengeable solution to the problem. Thomas's incorrigibility explanation is fine as far as it goes and as long as there is a referent to which one can defer: but it dissolves in the face of the ubiquity of the sign. At the limit, Thomas needs to appeal to a reality separate from the sign to point to his incorrigibility problem. Take away that reality and his explanation dissolves with it.

Thus in this approach to poststructuralism we have lost not just the referent but also the signified. There is just a world of signifiers beyond which we cannot pass. These signifiers take on meaning not just through Saussurean difference but through what Derrida calls *différance*. This is a word he has coined himself to conflate two things: difference, which is synchronic and spatial, and "deferring", in the sense of putting off in time. Thus by signifying, the sign takes on a meaning for the present that denies other meanings. Yet this cannot be permanent; another meaning is always waiting in the wings. Moreover, by uttering one signifier, one excludes for the present the uttering of another signifier. That will be deferred until later, when once more there is space for it.

Hence in writing, the concept of *différance*, as Weedon has pointed out, has immanently attacked the metaphysics of presence, in which the speaking subject's intention guarantees meaning, and language is a tool for expressing something beyond it. Now language has taken over precedence, and in doing so has decentred the speaking or writing subject. We no longer have the tyranny of the *logos* (roughly, law) of the author of either speech or written text.

Derrida's deconstruction, then, uses these ideas to undermine the origins and essence of existence. He points out that too many systems of meaning are constructed on a basis of binary opposition, in which one thing is always privileged over another, and discourse takes its meaning from this binary opposition. As Ryan puts it

> The second term in each case is inevitably made out to be external, derivative, and accidental in relation to the first, which is either an ideal limit or the central term of the metaphysical system . . . [because] the second term in each case usually connotes something that endangers the values the first term assures, values that connote presence, proximity, ownership, property, identity, truth conceived as conscious mastery, living experience, and a plenitude of meaning. The second terms usually suggest the breakup of all of these reassuring and empowering values, such terms as difference, absence, alteration, history, repetition, substitution, undecidability, and so on.
>
> (Ryan, 1982)

Deconstruction, in contrast, proceeds by indicating that what was excluded by the binary opposition as secondary and inferior can be shown to be more "primordial" than the original. In philosophical terms, whereas most metaphysical systems develop through seeking essences and origins that do not themselves depend on something prior, Derrida claims to have shown that this is a fruitless task, because all is only *différance*, and there are no such sole origins.

CONCLUSIONS

There are none.

DISCUSSION QUESTIONS

1. Write out, in your own words, Foucault's claim about the nature of truth. Now consider the following sentence from a management report: "The materials variance this month

was £210,000." Is this truth conditional on the system of thought of the industrialized twentieth century? Is this what Foucault was referring to when discussing "truth"?

2. We stated above that "Foucault argues that power is an integral component in the production of truth." Does this mean that the variance in question 1 above is what it is just because management has power over others and says that is what it is?

3. Miller and O'Leary analyse the growth of cost accounting control systems. Contrast (or compare) their analysis with the discussions in Chapter 4 of the work of Hopper, Storey and Willmott, and particularly the latter's reference to Clawson.

4. Here are some signifiers: variance, efficiency, overhead, control. How might you identify the signifieds and referents of these? Are there referents to them, indeed?

5. We wrote above that "the sign is the reality: and there is no space for suggesting any other reality". Illustrate this with reference to managerial discussions over cutting wastage, maximizing profits, and "imposing the disciplines of the market-place".

6. Think carefully what you mean by cost control in today's environment. Now try to envisage cost control on a fourteenth-century serf's landholding. Does the term have any meaning in this context, and if so, what? What does this tell you about the notion of "systems of thought"?

7. Poststructuralism may seem to conclude that there is no single understanding to be drawn from a passage of writing. Consider this in the context of (a) a report on expected costs in a new factory and (b) this chapter. Can you go back to the author in either case to fix the meaning of the words? Should you do so?

6

There's a Lot Going On Out There and This Has Been Just Some Of It

> One thing about pioneers that you don't hear mentioned is that they are invariably, by their nature, mess-makers. They go forging ahead, seeing only their noble, distant goal, and never notice any of the crud and debris they leave behind them.
>
> – Robert Pirsig

In this final chapter, I shall abandon what has, I hope, been a muted personal voice and be more open in judging the ideas contained in the previous chapters. I do this within a context that will also raise some theoretical ideas not otherwise covered up to now; and also in the context of the phenomenon of postmodernism, which has dominated cultural studies for the past few years.

If we ask why the ideas contained in Chapters 2–5 have arisen, a number of plausible reasons may present themselves. With the exception of the contingency approaches in Chapter 2, most of the work has been UK-based (or undertaken by those in North America with their theoretical roots in the UK). In the absence of the strait-jacket imposed by US doctoral programmes, which heavily restricted investigations to conventional topics and restricted methodology to neoclassical economics (within which I include property rights/agency/transaction cost models) there was a freedom to explore insights from other areas of social science. This was perhaps infused also by the invitations to radicality that followed the events of 1968; by the willingness of social scientists not trained in either accounting or economics to co-operate in asking questions about accounting; and by the existence of a UK journal (*Accounting, Organizations and Society*) which was willing to publish broader-based research. All of this is supposition, and need not be pursued in any detail.

But one further factor must be pursued: the theoretical bankruptcy of conventional approaches to management accounting. Over the period from the 1960s to the mid-1980s, there was a very clear split between that part of management accounting research that concentrated on the practice of management accounting – for example, surveys of the use of management accounting techniques, particularly budgetary control systems – and that which was undertaken and published in the higher-status US journals. The latter was replete with quantitative models that demonstrated the mathematical facility of their authors and were often remarkably elegant; but they were highly rationalistic, and made heroic assumptions about people's ability to make complex computational calculations at the same time that they assumed the most simple models conceivable of human utility and purpose. This arid economism broke down in the mid-1980s when it became clear that the world of practice was completely uninterested, and the refinement of techniques had reached a stage of rarification where a small number of researchers were, in effect, talking only to themselves.

It would of course be misleading to suggest that the four approaches we have considered in this book have superseded such work. With the possible exception of the systems approach, which makes the fewest implicit criticisms of conventional society and conventional theory, there has been little sign that mainstream management accounting research has recognized any fundamental flaw in rational economism. It has of course changed direction; we now have considerable interest in management accounting for new manufacturing technologies, strategic management accounting, and so on. Viewed by conventional researchers as revolutionary (or at the very least, highly evolutionary) such work may be seen from the point of view of this book to be little more than elaborations of previous studies.

We shall begin this final chapter with a brief review of the ideas of Chapters 2 to 5, confronting the schools of thought with each other and returning to the lacunae of traditional theory outlined in Chapter 1. Then we shall outline recent arguments concerning the claimed move from modernity to postmodernity. Against this backcloth we can then turn to the ideas of Jurgen Habermas. Habermas has stood out over the past few years as an eminent writer who has constructed a system against post-modernity and poststructuralism, which he has seen as a betrayal of the rationalist intent – a dangerous slide into proto-fascism in its unwillingness to confront the notion of social development. Habermas's ideas have been interpreted differently from author to author in the accounting literature. Some have viewed him as post-Marxist (see Laughlin, 1987, 1988; Power and Laughlin, 1992). Others, including myself, view him as neo-Marxist (cf. Puxty, 1991; Arrington and Puxty, 1991). His project, founded like many others on the significance of language and communication (though in a unique way), has irritated many more traditional radical thinkers, while being in direct conflict with French structuralist and poststructuralist approaches.

Finally, we shall offer a brief coda to consider where the debates we have outlined have brought us to.

SYSTEMS, INTERPRETATION, THE RADICAL AND THE RE-RADICALIZED

The systems of thought outlined in this book have differed in many ways, but a small number of key underlying beliefs and assumptions may be pinpointed. One such, that we have already touched on, is what has generally passed for a belief in rationality and progress. A systems approach is generally founded in the possible improvement in systems themselves. By positing a synchronic interdependency, systems theory proposes that harmony can be attained and maintained. This is not, of course, to suggest that there is no dynamic, nor that there is no conflict. In particular the cybernetics of Ross Ashby and Stafford Beer were founded in the belief that a revolution was needed to move away from static models, and the transition models of Ashby's *Introduction to Cybernetics* are founded wholly as models *for* change. A clearly valid criticism of systems theory is that ultimately it has no content, in that the universalist models presented are supposedly transcendental, and work across historical eras and across cultures. A content, of course, can arise from observation or from supplementary theorizing: but the abstract nature of the core theory of systems stands as a skeleton to be completed. This then may be extended to systems theories of organizations. The dynamics of the organizations are taken as a starting point, and then completed by inserting propositions about, for example, the political in a particular subenvironment. Left to themselves, the models of systems theory can also appear curiously static, because their only conception of change is change from outside, or change as a result of the initial programming of the system. Ashby has models of interconnected systems determining change in each other. Yet these changes cannot include any second-order feedbacks into the structures of the programming of the systems themselves. It is true that general and especially open systems theory does certainly permit learning through second-order feedbacks. The problem then becomes one of the reader's deciding whether they have faith in the essential wholeness of the social, economic and political milieu in which organizations and their accounting systems operate.

The Marxist project, indicating as it does that there is a dynamic within the contradictions of historical circumstances themselves, is in this sense an advance. The very core of the theory requires and explains the dynamics for change. The dialectic through which history unfolds itself acts as the driving force for change; this means that the theory itself incorporates as an intrinsic element the seeds of its own development, and at the same time, the seeds of social transformation. For management accounting, the change is significant. Systems theory and cybernetics permit the management accountant to observe the nature of the organization within which the prescribed systems operate, and to take the organizational structure as itself the systems skeleton within which the particular features of the individual organization can (albeit through dynamic homeostasis) experience change. Radical theory offers the probability that the very system within which management accounting is embedded is inherently unstable; and the management accounting system may well be one of the features that acts as part of the contradictions in the system that make it unstable. Homeostats under radical theory can only be localized; this means they do not constitute a totality; it follows that, despite the models of loose coupling that characterize analyses of dispersed social systems, they do not have any means of predicting change as such.[1] However, this is not to suggest that radical theory has a complete set of tools for understanding at the localized level. Marxist theory does not, in itself, offer ways of identifying those features of a social or organizational system that might act as

---

[1] That is, the mixture of the localized homeostat and loose coupling permits of unexplained change, but cannot incorporate it as intrinsic.

legitimators and hence barriers to change, and those features that are sufficiently immanently contradictory to act as a driver for change. Nevertheless it provides the initial tools for the reconstitution of what dynamic processes might act as drivers across the organization.

Particularistic as it is, interpretation theory shares with the systems approach an inherent conservatism. Both are operable in a static equilibrium; both lack any social dynamics. Interpretation theory does of course have a microdynamic in the individual confrontation, and in the development of negotiated understandings among participating individuals. It does not have a macro-dynamic, and just as it has been criticized for its inability to explain the social more generally (how do you get to society from the individual and the group?) it must accordingly lack a social dynamic.

On the face of it, Foucauldian analysis avoids these difficulties, both by bypassing *Verstehen* to consider the particularities of a given system of thought, and likewise by denying systematicity to its ontology. In terms of the totality of Foucault's project, this presents us with a difficulty. Either his theory is a grand theory or it is not. He assures us that it is not, as we saw in the last chapter. He does not claim a general theory of discontinuity, he says, and does not claim that discontinuity is necessarily character-istic of systems of thought. Some systems may be – some may not. Yet his schema is in direct contrast to systems theory, which is founded in an essential wholeness, even though the object of analysis may itself be loosely coupled. The epistemological difficulty for Foucault is then this: if his thought claims to be consistent, then it is itself a system and presumably then a grand theory; whereas if it is not, he provides no warrant for us to take any of his observations of conceptions as anything other than anecdotal. This point is echoed in different ways by Rorty (1986), and extended by Philp (1985), who seems to be applying analytic method to the problem:

> we should note that Foucault's claim that truth is merely what counts as true within a discourse is not easy to accept. If what Foucault says is true, then truth is always relative to discourse; there cannot be any statements which are true in all discourses, nor can there be any statements which are true for all discourses – so that, on Foucault's own account, what he says cannot be true!
>
> (Philp, 1985, p. 70)

However, this may be unfair to Foucault. What is shared by the systems, interpretive and radical approaches is a search for truth in a fairly conventional sense. They are asking how systems actually work, or what really happens in an encounter or what transcendent truth may be unmasked through tearing away the veil of ideology. But the poststructuralists can quite reasonably reply that any response such as this is already locked into an epistemology that is grounded in the ontology of consciousness, rather than the superstructural relativism of language. Once the rug has been pulled from under the feet of epistemology, we are left only with a decentred discourse that is ripe for further deconstruction. As such, the will to truth necessarily supplants the search for truth.

Conventional discourse tells us that management accounting has always seen itself as a rational project, one that enables an intentional management to control internal and external variables so as to achieve the success of the organizational system. Implicit in this, too, of course, is a political driver. The organization is embedded in an advanced capitalist society and as such must seek survival and growth through profit. How we view the operation of management control through the techniques of management accounting will depend on how we view both the society in which the accounting flourishes and the method appropriate to making sense of it. Systems theory, interactionism and radical theorizing all permit us to acknowledge the self-defined goals of management accounting. It is poststructuralism alone that cuts this ground from under our feet and demands that we perceive management accounting practices in a different light: most remarkably as a self-referential discourse grounded in the mutual self-referentiality of the simulacrum. If, as we shall shortly argue, our culture has now tacitly accepted the disappearance of rationality and progress, then the anchoring point of the referent will unsurprisingly have dissolved too. Whether or not cost and budget systems until recently truly constituted a discourse about reality, they can no longer do so.[2]

---

[2] An interesting example from the UK over the past ten years has been the demand by the government for value-for-money in the public sector. This has never been satisfactorily defined as relating to *what is*, and as a discourse about simulacra it could not be. The application of accountants' measuring methods by accountants (particularly large audit firms as consultants) to the ambiguity of phenomena such as quality of service, indicates that the whole discourse was severely problematic. A further example would be the mandated use by the state sector of government targets for levels of inflation as what was actually expected in designing their budgets and forecasts. Since nobody believed the targets would

BACK TO THE TRADITIONAL PARADIGM

At this point we return to Chapter 1, in which we listed a number of characteristics of traditional management accounting theory that were taken as self-evident, yet would be called into question by the paradigms considered here. Those characteristics were: it is framed from the perspective of the organization; it supposes the organization to be effectively a closed system; it has a technical orientation; it is prescriptive, ahistorical, apolitical, rationalistic, functionalist, reductionist, and positivist; and it is problem-centred. Let us return to these now to see how they have been reconstituted or undermined by our alternative ways of seeing management accounting.

To begin with, the ideas in this book have progressed steadily away from the prescriptive orientation of traditional theory. The abandonment of technicism goes hand in hand with the abandonment of the organization's own perspective. Once we turn to view the organization and its control systems in a broader context we lose the purpose of improvement and efficiency and, indeed, with the radical turn we reconstruct the drive for efficiency politically as part of a system of exploitation. Only the systems approach takes on the organization's perspective, and only then under certain conditions. Systems theory can be used instrumentally in this way: but it is not immanent to the perspective itself. Some likewise believe that through interactionism they can better understand the operation of managerial systems so as to enhance them. Enhancement of course has to be based on criteria, and we may assume that although some of the criteria may give the impression of enhancing social cohesion, the radical perspective cautions us to take care. Those controlling the entry of improvement methods thereby control how they are used, and in the profit-making organization it is unlikely they will be used to enhance the quality of life of employees to the detriment of the owners. However, it has to be acknowledged that in themselves interpretive approaches are not open-system as systems theory understands this. Radical theory is, and perceives the way in which the structures beyond the confines of the organization permeate its control system both in terms of their mode of operation and their purposes. Class systems are reflected in

be attained, the whole exercise bore no relation to "actuality". But with Baudrillard we may begin to wonder if that actuality exists as the rhetoric implies, or whether we do indeed have a self-referential discourse.

managerial hierarchies. Exploitation is reflected in the ownership structure. Contradictions in society beyond the organization mesh with contradictions within it. However, with poststructuralism we find more difficult ground and indeed, it may be argued that the language we are using is simply inapplicable to the poststructuralist understanding of the control system. To the extent that "open system" means that the relationship between features within the organization and features of society beyond it is recognized, then clearly Foucault may be said to recognize the openness. Beyond this, however, we cannot go, since systematicity in this sense is alien to Foucault's project. The calculative practices within organizations are argued to constitute part of society's other calculative practices. However, the organization's *boundary* is not in itself significant – that is, the reflection of practice from within to practice outside the organization is irrelevant – and hence the reference to the openness of the system is outside the recognized discourse.

We turn next to other features of traditional theory. It is, we have suggested, ahistorical and apolitical. As to the first, it hardly needs repeating that a historical trace is fundamental to Marxism; and as we have seen, the Foucauldian approach in a very different way considers historical periods. However, this "different way" changes the whole nature of what we mean by being historical, because by acknowledging historical disjunctures, it fails to provide a fully longitudinal trace that might be argued to constitute historical explanation. As to systems theory and interpretation, both lack the historical element as traditional theory does. Turning to the political, again, no comment need be made of the centrality of the political to radical theory. Generally, interpretation theory is likewise argued to lack any explicit recognition of the political in any except the most localized sense. However, more needs to be said about systems theory and poststructuralism in the political context.

First, let us consider the politics of systems theory. We argue here that any lack of explicit political context may generally be taken to constitute a conservative stance. The very lack of any explicit consideration of change necessarily implies, by omission, an acceptance of the status quo. Most commentators have argued that systems theory is inherently conservative because, to the extent that it is wholly an abstract general systems theory, it takes no political position; and to the extent that it is organic open systems theory, it relies heavily on the concept of homeostasis which, it is argued, leads to equilibrium. Success in achieving equilibrium is incompatible with the inherent contradictions of social dynamics under Marxism: and hence, either way, systems theory is conservative. In the management control context, this is illustrated by not only the instrumentalism that we have discussed already, in which managers can use systems concepts to keep their organizations in control, but also by the *direction* taken by systems researchers, who investigate disturbances to systems as if they were unquestionably exceptional, with equilibrium and hence continuity of the current system being the norm. We might argue that they have been seduced by the rhetoric of cohesion and order. But this direction of research can be questioned, if we extend somewhat the notion of system. Systematicity is, of course, fundamental to many philosophers; and although Hegel was a highly conservative philosopher politically, this was not true of Marx. Was Marx then a systems theorist? Arguably so, for he was concerned with systemic interactions, and with systemic change – and his conceptual framework emphasized holism. This, of course, extends the bounds of systems theory beyond the structures we considered in Chapter 2. There is nothing wrong with that.

Turning secondly to the politics of poststructuralism, we again find a complex situation. Poststructuralism is in so many ways the reverse of systems theory. In particular, its whole intent is to *disrupt*. It disrupts the way we think about our world, and it is arguably concerned thereby with disrupting the world itself. Foucault disrupts the idea of transhistorical continuity and progress; Derrida disrupts the power of logos; and Baudrillard disrupts practically everything. This disruption is itself immanently political. It is not conservative, for conservatism is about conserving, and disruption necessarily undermines conservation. All the French thinkers we have met began from Marx, but then reconstituted his project severely, so much so that arguably there was little left that was recognizable. Thus towards the end of his life Foucault affirmed that:

> It is impossible at the present time to write history without using
> a whole range of concepts directly or indirectly linked to Marx's
> thought and situating oneself within a horizon of thought which
> has been defined and described by Marx.
>
> (Foucault, 1980, p. 53)

Yet his whole historical position was itself set to disrupt Marx as much as conservative thinking, for Marx's history, albeit one of periodization and change in social configurations from period to period, was one of progress and development. Foucault's history denies this. Derrida similarly insists on his radicalism in interview;

yet his concepts may be used to disrupt radicalism itself. Baudrillard's case is especially curious. Beginning as a Marxist, he then challenged Marx (or, some would say, a caricature of Marx), and then challenged everything else.

And yet the treatment of their ideas may be interpreted as conservative within the accounting literature (see Moore, 1991 on accounting scholars' treatment of Foucault's ideas, for example). Whereas the radical accounting literature is clear in its intentions, the growing number of poststructuralists show little sign of any political engagement. This is as true of Arrington and Francis (1989) as it is of, say, Miller and O'Leary (1987) and Hoskin and Macve (1986). However, care must be taken here. There is no compulsion on the part of such writers to be politically engaged, as long as they acknowledge that they are ploughing their own particular furrow in accounting and drawing on poststructuralist insights; they become amenable to critique only when they make claims to be importing a method into accounting when many commentators on the original framework of ideas claim these ideas are indeed politically engaged in a way that has vanished in the transition to accounting.

Returning to some of the other characteristics of traditional theory (that they are rationalistic, reductionist, functionalist, positivist, and problem-centred), we may deal briefly with most of them. Systems theory is clearly rationalistic; none of the others are, although the radical turn has its own very different rationale. Only interactionism could reasonably stand accused of being reductionist, and I think there is no defence to that.[3]

Systems theory again might be accused of functionalism, and insofar as it is standard open-systems contingency theory, I think this is justified. The features of the environment identified in contingency theories of management control and the features of the control system do show signs of being treated as related through a functional relationship. There are hints of this functional relationship, too, in interpretive studies; and some have accused certain schools of Marxism as having functionalist tendencies.[4]

---

[3] Of course the very language of "defence" imposes a supposed criticism. Interpretive studies are proudly reductionist in the sense that they contend that it is only through the particularistic interaction that sense may be made of social encounters and hence of the way we make sense of our world. This is the problematic they have set, and the framework they have built is in many ways an admirable one.

[4] This can happen when, for instance, superstructural phenomena are identified in terms of the functions they perform for a ruling class. Their existence and reproduction relies on the class structure and hence is functional for it.

Systems theory is not positivist in the strictest Machian sense, since it relies on holistic explanation that necessarily involves unobservables; however, many elements of management accounting uses of systems concepts do tend to be positivist in their approach to evidence and the interpretation of evidence. Foucault, too, has been said to be positivist, since he relies heavily on the evidence available to him in the records, eschewing webs of *necessary* links among the phenomena he observes. Finally, in the managerial sense, only systems theory is clearly problem-orientated, although once again one use of interpretive studies may be employed in that way.

We have now reached a stage where we can turn from our review of where we have been so far to our final consideration of the framework within which social theories compete for space; and this raises the issue of modernity and postmodernity. We can then turn to our final theorist, Habermas, in the context of postmodernity and the struggle for rationalism in the face of the poststructuralist disruption.

MODERNISM AND POSTMODERNISM

There is no agreement on what modernism and postmodernism mean; or whether indeed they are the same as modernity and postmodernity (we shall follow here those writers who suggest the terms may be used interchangeably). The project of modernity is generally agreed to have started around the time of the enlightenment, when science bloomed, taking over from religious authority as the socially-accepted fount of knowledge; at the same time, social and political ideas of the significance of the individual underwent a revolution. It is often not realized that, before this period, the individual as an independent, thinking unit was not common either to formal philosophy or to common understanding (we discussed this in Chapter 1). From the enlightenment came, of course, the seeds of ideas of personal liberty that were to be slogans in both the French Revolution and the American War of Independence; and which were subsequently to lead to the formulation of the utility function that underlies all neoclassical economics today.

The project of modernity brought hope. There was a belief in the perfectibility of the individual and of the political system. In criticizing the divine right of kings and the authority of the church in secular matters, it was believed that a better society could be designed; that political systems could hold out hope for individual liberty free of intolerance and the arbitrary exercise of authority: and that man could progress to a higher state. Throughout the nineteenth century this vision drove many on to reforms of social institutions, which in Britain meant political reform, prison reform, reform of the structure of and recruitment to the civil service, and the rise of professions to govern these new institutions based on knowledge and expertise instead of birthright and social standing. Although many of the results fell far short of the ideal, nevertheless there was a general belief in progress and that this would continue.

Many argue that this project of modernity died with the Holocaust. There was, simply, no room within a notion of the gradual improvement of social institutions and human personal development for institutionalized genocide. This did not destroy modernity in the cultural understanding of the public, but it did sow the seeds for the breakdown of the project of modernity.

In its place, over the past decade or so, has come the period that is now called postmodern (many of these terms are taken from the arts). To take just a few examples: the clear line of progress in painting from representational art through the Chagall–Picasso attempt to break down the constraints of representation through to abstract art, a progress that lasted until at least the 1960s, has now fragmented into many schools. The development of music from the rigid patterns of the classical form through to the breakdown of simple form in the romantic period, followed by the breakdown of tonality in the twentieth century, has been followed by a period when tonality has made a resurgence alongside atonality, with the rise of minimalism providing a challenge from an entirely new direction. Architecture, too, has seen the modernist progress from ornamental to functional buildings, from buildings as art to buildings as machines, collapse under the weight of criticism. In the political sphere the certainty of finding the right political system, common to both socialist countries and those with market economies, has broken down as the former have collapsed under the weight of structural inefficiencies and the latter have undergone successive economic and political crises. There is no longer any clear hierarchy, it is argued. As a society, we no longer acknowledge the movie of the *auteur* as superior to the Hollywood blockbuster; music that takes months to write as superior to the popular song; art warranted as serious by the art critics as superior to a reproduction depicting a sorrowful child with one glistening tear. The old certainties have collapsed; and as Lyotard put it in a well-known phrase, we have "lost the nostalgia for the grand narrative".

This, at least as much as anything else, may explain the loss of faith in the appropriateness to management accounting of the economic and operational research models of yesterday. As we have lost faith in human rationality, so mathematical models based on rationality have appeared increasingly out of touch. As we have lost faith in the grand narrative, the project to create a grand theory for management accounting has ground to a halt: we no longer believe that through continued model building we can reach a synthesis of knowledge with which to instruct the practitioner in the "right way" to design or use management accounting systems.

The traditional economistic model has reflected this by turning to agency theory. Agency theory is proudly proclaimed to be "non-normative". It does not tell practitioners what to do. We can rephrase this: it holds out no hope for systematic improvement. Scholars working within the agency paradigm have abandoned any attempt to evaluate systems, concentrating instead on a libertarian–conservative analysis of the way certain economic relations point in terms of human behaviour. It is, perhaps, even more arid and lacking in content than systems theory. The world depicted by agency theory is one in which there are no asymmetries of power, for everyone has an equal opportunity to contract. There are no organizations in a meaningful sense, according to Fama, only clusters of contracts. There are no people, only contracting parties. This abandonment of the field is, it could be argued, precisely what we would expect from a postmodern accounting. It is an accounting corresponding to Philip Glass's music.

But there is a disturbing undercurrent to all this. We have described part of the postmodern turn as being concerned with the breakdown of a faith in rationality. The models of Chapters 2 and 4 are essentially rationalistic. They are built on the propositions of coherence among different parts of systems, and on either actual or intended rationality on the part of individuals. Radical theory may have acknowledged the significance of the sign in the development of cultural ideologies: but it still does so within a paradigm which supposes that a rationality beyond the level of ideology is possible. The interpretive movement of Chapter 3, on the other hand, rooted though it is in ideas developed before the Second World War, appears to be more consistent with postmodernity in that, in most interpretations at least, it has abandoned the field of the grand synthesis for the project of suggesting that it is only through the individual interpretive encounter and the constructions that arise from it that social activities can be understood. More radically, the poststructuralist ideas that were outlined in Chapter 5 have abandoned quite explicitly any pretence at a grand narrative: either through the discontinuity of systems of thought, or the lack of total coherence of the individual text or social phenomenon.

THE POSSIBILITY OF RADICAL RECONSTRUCTION: HABERMAS

There have been two clearly opposed readings of the challenge to modernity. These are elegantly expressed by Turner:

> If one believes that traditional society was based on hierarchy, inequality and violence, then the modernist critique of tradition is progressive. If, however, one regards the gas chambers as the final resting point of modernization, then postmodern objections to modern instrumental rationalism are progressive.
>
> (Turner, 1990, p. 10)

In Chapter 5 we have seen at length the direction in which poststructuralism has taken us. Key features have been its disruption of logos and its challenge to modernity through the freeing of the signifier. Severed from the referent or even from the signified, this has raised doubts about the rationalism of the systems we come across and, crucially, the possible rationalisms that might replace the old systems. There are many interlinked systems we may be concerned with – political systems, social systems, legal systems, intellectual systems, systems of scientific thought, moral systems, and in their own small way, managerial systems – and the exploding of these in postmodernity leaves the possibility that no certainty is offered in return. We cannot trace our way through the maze of these supposedly interconnected systems, because parts have gone missing, and this in turn means a decentring of rationalism. What hope is left? One scholar who has taken this question seriously is Jurgen Habermas. He began his massive project to reconstitute our rationality long before the problem of postmodernity emerged in our intellectual discourse, and he has become perhaps the most eminent critic of the tendency to postmodernity. Postmodernity leads to a mess, he suggests; he suggests, too, a way out.

To rescue modernity we need to be clearer about its nature; a means to interrogate this is to turn back to the dawn of the age of modernity and ask about its emergence from a previous era.

The pre-modern world was one in which religion, magic and myth were intertwined. Habermas quotes Weiss as characterizing the break from this period as "thinking through to the end of given meaning or value contents [which implies] both going back to the ultimate basic principles and developing the further consequences or the totality of implications" (Habermas, 1984, p. 176). Faith cannot do this, since it cannot ask about means–ends or reasons why, since ultimately it must accept divine necessity as a sufficient explanation. On the face of it this means we are in the conventional territory of viewing the key event as the supplanting of myth/faith/religious belief with rationality. But Habermas does not see rationality as such as the characteristic that announces modernity. Instead it is the differentiation process, whereby the consciousness of people within traditional forms of society develop relatively autonomous spheres of culture. These spheres are the natural, social, and subjective worlds. As the descendants of modernity, we take the difference among these for granted. For instance, how my friendship develops with you is quite separate from the way science develops theories about physical phenomena.

Habermas argues that the key to modernity is the recognition of the differentiation among these three spheres, each of which develops in its own way. This is illustrated in Table 6.1.

TABLE 6.1 Habermas's three cultural spheres.

Cultural spheres	Natural world	Social world	Subjective world
Corresponding practice	Science	Politics, morality, law	Art, literature
Rationalization process	Instrumental reason	Practical reason	Affective reason

Briefly, reading down columns 2–4, we find, first, a world of natural phenomena, the subject of science and technology (including accounting), which develops through instrumental reason. It is a means–end rationality. We wish to achieve something – especially, control over the physical world. Second, there is a social world, where people interact and struggle over rights and justice. The appropriate mode of reasoning, Habermas suggests here, is quite different from instrumental reason. For instance, when considering a wage claim, instrumental reason would look to markets; practical reason would look to a notion such as fairness. Third, there is the subjective world, which must ultimately rely on personal and private judgements about aesthetics.

Thus these spheres became separated in modernity; and in itself that is unproblematic. But when we ask how problems within each sphere are interrogated, and progress is made, the answer must be: through cognitive/communicative structures. Each of the three spheres can only be institutionalized and furthered through argument. Science/technology constitutes a discursive practice (using language about a certain conception of truth about the physical world); so do politics (using different intellectual arguments with different criteria); and similarly for the world of art, where there is a discourse of pleasure and enjoyment in the public sphere. These are different discourses, but each also depends on its own conceptions of truth. These in turn revolve around Habermas's theory of communicative competence; because all developments are the results of action (cf. symbolic interactionism's insistence, which we discussed in Chapter 3, that society only exists through action) and speech is one particular and special form of action.

Habermas and communicative competence

Leaving aside the personal world of the artistic, Habermas argues that society develops in the two spheres described above. One is the level of technological innovation and labour, an economic level which is concerned with man's relationship to the natural world. The second level is that of human interaction. The two levels are related, though independent. Labour is fundamental in the economic process, and hence the employment relation is necessarily one of exploitation. However, it is not claimed that the political and social superstructure is as a result derivative of and dependent on that process. The sphere of human interaction has its own laws of development.

A key feature of the social world, which mirrors exploitation at the economic level, is the domination of some classes by others. This domination is characterized through, embodied in, sustained by, and legitimized by, the communicative structures of society. Hence, to understand how this dominance relation operates, and its implications for human interaction as well as social structure, it is necessary to enquire into the linguistic process itself.

From this, an analysis of communication as a series of speech acts is necessary (this notion is developed from the work of Austin and Searle). Communication takes place because there are shared meanings of the symbols of speech. However, these shared meanings themselves result from the ideologically distorted structure of society: "the 'common accord' is not so much the prior condition of communication but rather the ultimate conclusion" (Thompson, 1982, p. 117).

Hence, to reach a genuine understanding and truth, undistorted by the normal basis of everyday speech, enquiry has to be made into the validity basis of speech. It is this which Habermas calls *universal pragmatics*; and it is from this that the four tests for the validity of speech acts are derived. General everyday speech is embedded in the matrix of the current dominational social structure. As such it will normally fail these conditions. Habermas does, however, define a special kind of speech act which he designates *discourse*. This is contrasted with everyday speech, which is designated as *action*. Discourse is speech which is specifically designed to reach an understanding. "The participants of a discourse are concerned, not to perform actions or to share experiences, but rather to search for arguments and justifications; and the only motive allowed in this search is 'a co-operative readiness to arrive at an understanding'" (Thompson, 1982, p. 119).

There are four conditions for valid discourse, which Habermas argues underlie all propositions made. These are that an utterer of statements is claiming to be:

1. uttering something understandably;
2. giving [the hearer] something to understand
3. making himself thereby understandable; and
4. coming to an understanding with another person.

As a result, he says, we claim to say something comprehensible, so we can be understood; we make the claim to a true propositional content; we wish to express our intentions truthfully so that our statement can be trusted; and finally, the statement must be made within the context of a shared normative background. He also makes the point that, in communicating, we assume a background consensus. Many interpretations are taken for granted. Habermas helpfully sums up this system as shown in Table 6.2. The ultimate intention of this is to provide a mechanism by which the domination inherent in social structure might be dissolved:

> Domination is. . .conceived as a systematic distortion of interaction or language; and the interest in emancipation becomes an interest in the transcendence of such structures of communication. . .
> Accordingly, systematically distorted communication is seen as the condition of the emancipatory interest: the interest only develops

TABLE 6.2 Habermas's interpretations of communication.

Domains of reality	Modes of communication: basic attitudes	Validy claims	General functions of speech
The world of external nature	Cognitive: objectivating attitude	Truth	Representation of facts
Our world of society	Interactive: conformative attitude	Rightness	Establishment of legitimate interpersonal relations
My world of internal nature	Expressive: expressive attitude	Truthfulness	Disclosure of speaker's subjectivity
Language	—	Comprehensibility	—

to the extent that domination is institutionalized. (Whether or not the empirical conditions will exist for the realization of undistorted communication is, in Habermas's opinion, an open question.)

(Held, 1980, p. 319)

Hence it will be seen that the mechanism for such dissolution is not one in which a Utopian social engineer designs a "better" social structure: it is one in which society itself becomes involved, through discourse, in a course of self-discovery and emancipation. Habermas compares this to Freudian psychoanalysis, in which the patient and the analyst working together may both be able to recognize what is wrong. However, the analyst cannot just prescribe, in the way the physical medical practitioner can. Nor can the patient, however much he or she has read about psychoanalysis, cure themselves. Knowing you are a depressive does not enable you to avoid depression. But, once the situation is understood by both parties, a process can take place that will enable a patient to become cured. The analogy with society is proposed by Habermas. Pointing to social ills will not cure them. Only a process that dissolves domination through linguistic structures can do this.

These, then, are the ways in modernity that an ideal discourse might take place. But Habermas acknowledges that there has been a distortion to the development of the modern world. To understand this we need to explain a further concept: that of the *lifeworld*. This is the world of our everyday experience, ramified with our past experiences. It "stores the interpretive work of preceding generations". Thus communicative actions may add to this store; they may also challenge it. However, the three spheres we outlined earlier in Table 6.1 gain their own autonomy. Instrumental sciences such as economics and accounting are systems of thinking and action that develop a life of their own; and Habermas perceives a danger that these systemic and instrumental structures begin to colonize the lifeworld. As Power and Laughlin phrase it, "Guided by the steering media of 'money' and 'power' the domain of instrumental reason has come to smother and eclipse both the lifeworld and other possible orders of reasoning e.g. politics and subjectivity" (Power and Laughlin, 1992, p. 123). They then quote Habermas:

> The thesis of internal colonization states that the subsystems of the economy and the state become more and more complex as a consequence of capitalist growth and penetrate ever deeper into the symbolic reproduction of the lifeworld.
>
> (Habermas, 1987, p. 367)

Thus it may be that by setting up the criterion of ideal speech (whether or not it can be an actuality under capitalism), we have a touchstone by which to judge progress into defying this colonization; and the rationality of modernity can thereby be recovered.

Although clearly we cannot expend further space on these difficult ideas, one or two final points may be made in the context of poststructuralism and postmodernism. In the former case it will be seen why Habermas disagrees so fundamentally with the French thinkers. He conceives of the possibility of a transcendental truth through communicative action, whereas they raise major difficulties, Foucault for example seeing it as contingent on systems of thought and power. Habermas's project attempts to save the progress, systematicity and rationalism of modernity from the implicit helplessness of postmodernity.

(NOT) CONCLUSIONS

It is tempting at the end of over 100 pages of exposition to attempt to synthesize the stage we have reached and to draw some conclusions. But it is even more tempting not to do so, and I shall take the latter course. Someone once said words to the effect "if an argument can be summarized on the back of a cigarette packet, that is where it belongs". I agree. We have considered so many competing schools of thought – and competing thinkers within schools of thought – that to summarize would be presumptuous. So it is perhaps worth ending on a wistful note: namely, that if there are so many difficulties in philosophy and the social sciences beyond the relatively narrow world of accounting, it is scarcely surprising that accounting still has such a long road to travel in its search for truth and method.

DISCUSSION QUESTIONS

1. What do you understand Habermas to mean by the "lifeworld"? Is this the world envisaged by the interactionists of Chapter 3?
2. How might Habermas's critique of the colonization of the lifeworld by systems be interpreted in the light of the nature and purpose of management accounting systems?
3. What are the implications of the notion of postmodernity for (a) management control systems (b) theorizing management control systems?
4. Are you persuaded that the radical critique offers valid insights into the operation of management accounting?
5. In the light of your reading of this book as a whole, consider how (if at all!) your conceptions of cost and management accounting systems have changed.
6. After reading this book, do you believe you could construct accounting systems better? (Decide for yourself what "better" means for you.)

References

Amigoni, F. (1978). "Planning Management Control Systems", *Journal of Business Finance and Accounting*, Vol. 5(3), Autumn, pp. 279–91.

Anthony, R.N. (1965). *Planning and Control Systems: A Framework for Analysis*, Harvard University Press.

Anthony, R.N. (1988). *The Management Control Function*, Harvard University Press.

Armstrong, P. (1985). "Changing management control strategies: the role of competition between accountancy and other organizational professions", *Accounting, Organizations and Society*, Vol. 10(2), pp. 129–48.

Arnold, J. and Hope, T. (1983). *Accounting for Management Decisions*, Prentice-Hall.

Arrington, C.E. and Francis, J.R. (1989). "Letting the chat out of the bag: deconstruction, privilege and accounting research", *Accounting, Organizations and Society*, Vol. 14, pp. 1–28.

Arrington, C.E. and Puxty, A.G. (1991). "Accounting, Interests, and Rationality: A Communicative Relation", *Critical Perspectives in Accounting*, Vol. 2(1), pp. 31–58.

Ashby, W.R. (1955), "General Systems Theory as a New Discipline", address presented to the meeting of the Society for General Systems Research, Atlanta, Georgia, December.

Ashton, R.H. (1976). "Cognitive changes induced by accounting changes: experimental evidence on the functional fixation hypothesis". Supplement to *Journal of Accounting Research*, Vol. 1(17).

Bauman, Z. (1978). *Hermeneutics and Social Science*, Hutchinson.

Beer, S. (1962). "On Viable Governors", *Discovery*, October, pp. 39–44.

Bhaskar, K.N. (1981). "Quantitative aspects of management accounting". In Bromwich, M. and Hopwood, A.G. (eds), *Essays in British Accounting Research*, Pitman, pp. 229–73.

Blumer, H. (1969). *Symbolic Interactionism: Perspectives and Method*, Prentice-Hall.

Bougen, P. (1989). "The emergence, roles and consequences of an accounting-industrial relations interaction", *Accounting, Organizations and Society*, Vol. 14(3), pp. 203–34.

Boulding, K. (1956). "General Systems Theory – the Skeleton of Science", *Management Science*, April, pp. 197–208.

Bromwich, M. (1990). "The case for strategic management accounting: the role of accounting information for strategy in competitive markets", *Accounting, Organizations and Society*, Vol. 15(1/2), pp. 27–46.

151

Bruns, W. and Waterhouse, J.H. (1975). "Budgetary control and organization structure", *Journal of Accounting Research*, Vol. 13(2), Autumn, pp. 177–203.

Churchman, C.W. (1978). "Paradise regained: a hope for the future of systems design education", Keynote address, NATO workshop on systems science education. Gras-Ellenbach, February (unpublished).

Clawson, D. (1980). *Bureaucracy and the Labour Process*, Monthly Review Press.

Colville, I. (1981). "Reconstructing 'Behavioural Accounting'", *Accounting, Organizations and Society*, Vol. 6(2), pp. 119–32.

Cooper, C. and Puxty, A.G. (forthcoming (a)). "On the proliferation of accounting (his)tories", *Critical Perspectives in Accounting*.

Cooper, C. and Puxty, A.G. (forthcoming (b)). "Reading Accounting Writing", *Accounting, Organizations and Society*.

Cooper, D.J., Hayes, D. and Wolf, F. (1981). "Accounting in organized anarchies: understanding and designing accounting systems in ambiguous situations", *Accounting, Organizations and Society*, Vol. 6(3), pp. 175–91.

Cooper, R. and Kaplan, R. (1987). "How cost accounting distorts product costs". In Bruns, W.J. and Kaplan, R.S. (eds), *Accounting and Management: Field Study Perspectives*, Harvard Business School Press.

Craib, I. (1984). *Modern Social Theory*, Wheatsheaf.

Davidson, A.I. (1986). "Archaeology, Genealogy, Ethics", in Hay, D.C. (ed.), *Foucault: A Critical Reader*, Blackwell, pp. 221–33.

de Saussure, F. (1916). *Cours de linguistique générale* (trans. W. Baskin as *Course in General Linguistics*), Fontana, 1974.

Dent, J.F. (1986). "Organizational research in accounting: perspectives, issues and a commentary". In Bromwich, M. and Hopwood, A.G. (eds), *Research and Current Issues in Manaement Accounting*, Pitman, pp. 143–78.

Denzin, N. K. (1971). "Symbolic interactionism and ethnomethodology". In Douglas, J. (ed.), *Understanding Everyday Life*, Routledge and Kegan Paul, pp. 259–84.

Dreyfus, H.L. and Rabinow, P. (1982). *Michel Foucault: Beyond Structuralism and Hermeneutics*, Harvester.

Dyckman, T.R. (1981). "The intelligence of Ambiguity", *Accounting, Organizations and Society*, Vol. 6(4), pp. 291–300.

Earl, M.J. (1983). "Management information systems and management accounting". In D.J. Cooper, R. Scapens and J. Arnold (eds), *Management Accounting Research and Practice*, Institute of Cost and Management Accountants, pp. 22–72.

Earl, M.J. and Hopwood, A.G. (1980). "From management information to information management". In Lucas, H.C., Land, F.F., Lincoln, T.J. and Supper, K. (eds), *The Information Systems Environment*, North Holland.

Emmanuel, C. and Otley, D.T. (1985). *Accounting for Management Control*, Van Nostrand Reinhold.

Emmanuel, C., Otley, D.T. and Merchant, K. (1990). *Accounting for Management Control* (2nd edn), Chapman and Hall.

Ezzamel, M. and Hart, H. (1987). *Advanced Management Accounting: An Organizational Emphasis*, Cassell.

Flamholz, E.G., Das, T.K. and Tsui, A.S. (1985). "Toward an integrative framework of organizational control", *Accounting, Organizations and Society*, Vol. 10(1), pp. 35–50.

Foucault, M. (1961). *Folie et Déraison. Histoire de la Folie à l'âge classique* (trans. R. Howard as *Madness and Civilisation: A History of Insanity in the Age of Reason*), Tavistock, 1967.

Foucault, M. (1963). *The Birth of the Clinic*, Tavistock.

Foucault, M. (1966). *The Order of Things*, Tavistock.

Foucault, M. (1969). *The Archaeology of Knowledge*, Tavistock.

Foucault, M. (1975). *Discipline and Punish*, Penguin.

Foucault, M. (1976). *History of Sexuality*, Vol. 1, Penguin.

Foucault, M. (1980). *Power/Knowledge*, ed. Colin Gordon, Harvester.

Freud, S. (1920). *Beyond the Pleasure Principle*, Vol. 18, Standard Edition.

Garfinkel, H. (1967). *Studies in Ethnomethodology*, Prentice-Hall.

Giddens, A. (1976). *New Rules of Sociological Method*, Hutchinson.

Ginzberg, M.J. (1980). "An Organizational Contingencies View of Accounting and Information Systems Implementation", *Accounting, Organizations and Society*, Vol. 5(4), pp. 369–82.

Gordon, L.A. and Miller, D. (1976). "A contingency framework for the design of accounting information systems", *Accounting, Organizations and Society*, Vol. 1(1), June, pp. 59–69.

Gordon, L.A. and Narayanan, V.K. (1984). "Management accounting systems, perceived environmental uncertainty and organization structure: an empirical investigation", *Accounting, Organizations and Society*, Vol. 9(1), pp. 33–47.

Gurwitsch, A. (1966). *Studies in Phenomenology and Psychology*, Northwestern University Press.

Habermas, J. (1984). *The Theory of Communicative Action*, Vol. 1, Polity.

Habermas, J. (1987). *The Theory of Communicative Action*, Vol. 2, Polity.

Hacking, I. (1986). "The Archaeology of Foucault". In Hoy, D.C. (ed.), *Foucault: A Critical Reader*, Blackwell, pp. 27–40.

Harland, R. (1987). *Superstructuralism*, Routledge.

Hayes, D.C. (1977). "The contingency theory of managerial accounting", *The Accounting Review*, Vol. 52(1), January, pp. 22–39.

Hedberg, B.L.T. and Jönsson, S. (1978). "Design semi-confusing information systems for organizations in changing environments", *Accounting, Organizations and Society*, Vol. 3(1), pp. 47–64.

Held, D. (1980). *Introduction to Critical Theory*, Hutchinson.

Hicks, J.O. (1984). *Management Information Systems: A User Perspective*, West.

Hofstede, G. (1967). *The Game of Budget Control*, Tavistock.

Holloway, J. and Picciotto, S. (eds) (1978). *State and Capital: a Marxist Debate*, Arnold.

Hopper, T., Storey, J. and Willmott, H. (1987). "Accounting for accounting: towards the development of a dialectical view", *Accounting, Organizations and Society*, Vol. 12(5), pp. 437–56.

Hopwood, A.G. (1974). "Leadership Climate and the Use of Accounting Data in Performance Evaluation", *Accounting Review*, Vol. 49(3), pp. 485–95.

Hopwood, A.G. (1987). "The Archaeology of Accounting Systems", *Accounting, Organizations and Society*, Vol. 12(3), pp. 207–34.

Hoskin, K. and Macve, R. (1986). "Accounting and the examination: a genealogy of disciplinary power", *Accounting, Organizations and Society*, Vol. 11(2), pp. 105–36.

Hoskin, K. and Macve, R. (1988). "The Genesis of accountability: the West Point connections", *Accounting, Organizations and Society*, Vol. 13(1), pp. 37–73.

Hume, D. (1748). *An Enquiry Concerning Human Understanding*.

Jessop, B. (1982). *The Capitalist State*, Martin Robertson.

Johnson, H.T. and Kaplan, R.S. (1987). *Relevance Lost: The Rise and Fall of Management Accounting*, Harvard.

Jung, C.G. (1944). *Psychology and Alchemy*, Vol. 12, College Editions.

Katz, D. and Kahn, R.L. (1966). *The Social Psychology of Organizations*, Wiley.

Keynes, J.M. (1936). *The General Theory of Employment, Interest and Money*, Macmillan.

Kuhn, T.S. (1970). *The Structure of Scientific Revolutions*, University of Chicago Press.

Larrain, J. (1979). *The Concept of Ideology*, Hutchinson.

Lau, C.T. and Nelson, M. (1981). *Accounting Implications of Collective Bargaining*, Society of Management Accountants in Canada.

Laughlin, R.C. (1981). "On the nature of accounting methodology", *Journal of Business Finance and Accounting*, Vol. 8(3), pp. 329–51.

Laughlin, R.C. (1987). "Accounting systems in organizational contexts: a case for critical theory", *Accounting, Organizations and Society*, Vol. 12(5), pp. 479–502.

Laughlin, R.C. (1988). "Accounting in its social context: an analysis of the accounting systems of the Church of England", *Accounting, Auditing and Accountability*, Vol. 1(2), pp. 19–42.

Libby, R. (1981). *Accounting and Human Information Processing: Theory and Applications*, Prentice-Hall.

Litterer, J.A. (1969). *Organizations Vol. II: Systems, Control and Adaptation* (2nd edn), Wiley.

Loft, A. (1986). "Towards a critical understanding of accounting: the case of cost accounting in the UK, 1914–1925", *Accounting, Organizations and Society*, Vol. 11(2), pp. 137–69.

Lowe, E.A. and Tinker, A.M. (1977). "Siting the accounting problematic: towards an intellectual emancipation of accounting", *Journal of Business Finance and Accounting*, Vol. 4, pp. 263–76.

Mandel, E. (1969). *An Introduction to Marxist Economic Theory*, Merit Publishers.

March, J.G. (1987). "Ambiguity and accounting: the elusive link between information and decision making", *Accounting, Organizations and Society*, Vol. 12(2), pp. 153–68.

March, J.G. and Olsen, J.P. (1976). *Ambiguity, and Choice in Organizations*, Universitetsforlaget.

Markus, M.L. and Pfeffer, J. (1983). "Power and the design and implementation of accounting and control systems", *Accounting, Organizations and Society*, Vol. 8(2/3), pp. 205–18.

Marx, K. (1978). "The German Ideology". In Tucker, R.C. (ed.), *The Marx-Engels Reader* (2nd edn), Norton (original dated 1845–6).

Miller, P. and Napier, C. (1990). "How and why should we do the history of accounting?" Paper given at the conference "History of the Accounting Present", Denton, Texas, November.

Miller, P. and O'Leary, T. (1987). "Accounting and the Construction of the Governable Person", *Accounting Organizations and Society*, Vol. 12(3), pp. 235–65.

Mitroff, I.I. and Mason, R.O. (1983). "Can we design systems for managing messes? Or, why so many management information systems are uninformative", *Accounting, Organizations and Society*, Vol. 8(2/3), pp. 195–203.

Moore, D.C. (1991). "Accounting on trial: the critical legal studies movement and its lessons for radical accounting", *Accounting, Organizations and Society*, Vol. 16(8), pp. 763–93.

Nahapiet, J. (1988). "The rhetoric and reality of an accounting change: a study of resource allocation", *Accounting, Organizations and Society*, Vol. 13(4), pp. 333–58.

Neimark, M. and Tinker, T. (1986). "The social construction of management control systems", *Accounting, Organizations and Society*, Vol. 11(4/5), pp. 369–95.

Newman, E. (1949). *Wagner Nights*, Putnam.

Ogden, S. and Bougen, P. (1985). "A radical perspective on the disclosure of accounting information to trade unions", *Accounting, Organizations and Society*, Vol. 10(2), pp. 211–24.

Otley, D.T. (1980). "The Contingency Theory of Management Accounting: Achievement and Prognosis", *Accounting, Organizations and Society*, Vol. 5(4), pp. 413–28.

Outhwaite, W. (1975). *Understanding Social Life*, George Allen & Unwin.

Philp, M. (1985). "Michel Foucault". In Skinner, Q. (ed.), *The Return of Grand Theory in the Human Sciences*, Cambridge.

Poster, M. (1979). "Foucault's true discourses", *Humanities in Society*, Vol. 2(2).

Power, M. and Laughlin, R. (1992). "Critical Theory and Accounting". In M. Alvesson and H.C. Willmott (eds), *Critical Management Studies*, Sage.

Puxty, A.G. (1991). "Social Accountability and Universal Pragmatics", *Advances in Public Interest Accounting*, Vol. 4, pp. 35–45.

Roberts, J. (1989). "Authority or domination: Alternative possibilities for the practice of control". In Chua, W.F., Lowe, T. and Puxty, T. (eds), *Critical Perspectives in Management Control*, pp. 293–321.

Rockness, H.O. and Shields, M.D. (1984). "Organizational control systems in research and development", *Accounting, Organizations and Society*, Vol. 9(2), pp. 165–77.

Ronen, J. and Livingstone, J.L. (1975). "An expectancy theory approach to the motivational impacts of budgets", *Accounting Review*, Vol. 50(4), pp. 671–85.

Rorty, R. (1986). "Foucault and Epistemology". In Hoy, D.C. (ed.), *Foucault: A Critical Reader*, Blackwell, pp. 41–50.

Rosenberg, D. (1989). "Professional authority and resource allocation: treasurers and politics in UK local governments". In Chua, W.F., Lowe, T. and Puxty, T. (eds), *Critical Perspectives in Management Control*, MacMillan, pp. 293–321.

Rosenberg, D., Tomkins, C. and Day, P. (1982). "A work role perspective of accountants in local government service departments", *Accounting, Organizations and Society*, Vol 7(2), pp. 123–37.

Ryan, M. (1982). *Marxism and Deconstruction*, Johns Hopkins University Press.

Simmonds, K. (1981). "Strategic management accounting", *Management Accounting*, April, pp. 26–9.

Simons, R. (1987). "Accounting control systems and business strategy: an empirical analysis", *Accounting, Organizations and Society*, Vol. 12(4), pp. 357–74.

Sizer, J. (1989). *An Insight into Management Accounting*, Penguin.

Skidmore, W. (1979) *Theoretical Thinking in Sociology* (2nd edn), Cambridge.

Speight, H. (1960). *Economics: The Science of Prices and Incomes*, Methuen.

Stedry, A.C. (1960). *Budget Control and Cost Behavior*, Prentice-Hall.

Taylor, C. (1986). "Foucault on Freedom and Truth". In Hoy, D.C. (ed.), *Foucault: A Critical Reader*, Blackwell, pp. 69–102.

Thompson, J.B. (1982). "Universal Pragmatics". In Thompson, J.B. and Held, D. (eds), *Habermas: Critical Debates*, Macmillan, pp. 116–33.

Thompson, J. and Held, D. (eds) (1982). *Habermas: Critical Debates*, Macmillan.

Tinker, A.M. (1980). "Towards a Political Economy of Accounting", *Accounting Organizations and Society*, Vol. 5(1), pp. 147–60.

Tinker, A.M. (1984). "Theories of the State and the State of Accounting: Economic Reductionism and Political Voluntarism in Accounting Regulation Theory", *Journal of Accounting and Public Policy*, Vol. 3(1), pp. 55–74.

Tinker, A.M., Merino, B.D. and Neimark, M.D. (1982). "The normative origins of positive theories: ideology and accounting thought", *Accounting, Organizations and Society*, Vol. 7(2), pp. 167–200.

Tomkins, C. and Groves, R. (1983). "The everyday accountant and researching his reality", *Accounting, Organizations and Society*, Vol. 8(4), pp. 361–74.

Turner, B.S. (1990). "Periodization and politics in the postmodern". In Turner, B.S. (ed.), *Theories of Modernity and Postmodernity*, Sage, pp. 1–13.

von Bertalanffy, L. (1950). "The Theory of Open Systems in Physics and Biology", *Science*, Vol. 111, pp. 23–9.

Weick, K.E. (1979). *The Social Psychology of Organizing* (2nd edn), Addison Wesley.

Wells, A. (ed) (1978). *Contemporary Sociological Theories*, Goodyear.

White, S.K. (1988). *The Recent Work of Jurgen Habermas*, Cambridge.

Williams, J.J., Macintosh, N.B. and Moore, J.C. (1990). "Budget-related behavior in public sector organizations: some empirical evidence", *Accounting, Organizations and Society*, Vol. 15(3), pp. 221–46.

Willmott, H. (1983). "Paradigms for accounting research: critical reflections on Tomkins and Groves' 'Everyday accountant and researching his reality'", *Accounting, Organizations and Society*, Vol. 8(4), pp. 389–405.

Wilson, R.M.S. and Chua, W.F. (1988). *Managerial Accounting: Method and Meaning*, Van Nostrand Reinhold.

Index